Space Exploration
Reference
Library
Cumulative
Index

Space Exploration
Reference Library
Cumulative Index

Cumulates Indexes for:
Space Exploration: Almanac
Space Exploration: Biographies
Space Exploration: Primary Sources

Sarah Hermsen,
Index Coordinator

U·X·L
An imprint of Thomson Gale,
a part of The Thomson Corporation

Detroit • New York • San Francisco • San Diego • New Haven, Conn. • Waterville, Maine • London • Munich

Space Exploration: Cumulative Index

Project Editor
Sarah Hermsen

Product Design
Pamela Galbreath

Composition
Evi Seoud

Manufacturing
Rita Wimberley

Library of Congress Cataloging-in-Publication Data
Space exploration reference library. Cumulative index / Sarah Hermsen, index coordinator.
    p. cm.
    A cumulation of the indexes from Space exploration. Almanac; Space exploration.
Biographies; and Space exploration. Primary sources; grade level 5–12.
    ISBN 0-7876-9214-X (pbk.)
    1. Space exploration reference library—Indexes. 2. Astronautics—Juvenile literature—Indexes. 3. Astronautics—History—Encyclopedias, Juvenile—Indexes. 4. Outer space—Exploration—History—Encyclopedias, Juvenile—Indexes. I. Hermsen, Sarah.
    Z5061.S63 2004
    [TL788]
    016.6294—dc22   2004015882

Space Exploration Reference Library Cumulative Index

A1 = Space Exploration: Almanac, volume 1
A2 = Space Exploration: Almanac, volume 2
B = Space Exploration: Biographies
PS = Space Exploration: Primary Sources

A

AADSF. *See* Advanced Automated Directional Solidification Furnace (AADSF)

Aberration, chromatic
A: 2: 282–84

ABMA. *See* Army Ballistic Missile Agency (ABMA)

Accelerated expansion, of universe
A: 2: 314

Achromatic lens
A: 2: 283

Achromatic telescope
A: 2: 283

Ackmann, Martha, *PS: 74–89*
excerpts from *The Mercury 13: The Untold Story of Thirteen American Women and the Dream of Space Flight* (Ackmann), *PS: 79–86*

Action-reaction, Newton's law of
A: 1: 42–43, 53, 66–67

Adaptive optics
A: 2: 287

Address to the Nation on the Explosion of the Space Shuttle (Reagan)
PS: **139–41**

Advanced Automated Directional Solidification Furnace (AADSF)
B: 139

Advanced Satellite for Cosmology and Astrophysics (ASCA)
A: 2: 328

Advanced Space Propulsion Laboratory (Houston, Texas)
B: 57

Advanced X-Ray Astrophysics Facility
A: 2: 321–22
PS: 171, 172

Aeolipile (Hero's engine)
A: 1: 47

Aerodynamics
PS: 41

Aeronautics
PS: 40

Aeronautics, Tsiolkovsky, Konstantin, and
B: 193

Bold italic type indicates set titles. **Bold** type indicates main *Biographies* or *Primary Sources* entries, and their page numbers. Illustrations are marked by (ill.).

Aerospace industry, and space shuttle
PS: 124

AFIT. *See* Air Force Institute of Technology (AFIT)

A-4 rockets
A: 1: 79

African American astronauts
Bluford, Guy, *B:* 34–41
Cowings, Patricia, *B:* 119
Jemison, Mae, *B:* 37, 114–20
Lawrence, Robert Henry Jr., *B:* 37
McNair, Ronald, *B:* 42, 43 (ill.)

AFTE. *See* Autogenic Feedback Training Exercise (AFTE)

Agena spacecraft
A: 1: 154
B: 26

"Agreement Concerning Cooperation in the Exploration and Use of Outer Space for Peaceful Purposes"
A: 2: 196–97, 203, 205

Air Force Institute of Technology (AFIT)
B: 36

Air pressure, in Apollo-Soyuz test project
A: 2: 199–200

"Air Pressure on Surfaces Introduced into an Artificial Air Flow" (Tsiolkovsky)
B: 191
PS: 41

Aircraft. *See also* Experimental aircraft and spacecraft; specific aircraft
Tsiolkovsky's theories of, *B:* 190–91

Aircraft carriers, and jet planes
PS: 21

Aircraft, Tsiolkovsky's theories of
A: 1: 64
PS: 40–41

Aksenov, Vladimir
A: 2: 215 (ill.)

Alamogordo, New Mexico
A: 1: 96 (ill.), 97

Albertus Magnus, and gunpowder recipe
A: 1: 50

Aldridge, Peter
PS: 198

Aldrin, Edwin E. "Buzz," Jr., *A: 1:* 157, 178; *2:* 189; *B:* **1–10,** 2 (ill.), 7 (ill.), 9 (ill.), 28–30; *PS:* 46, 56, 72, 102, 104–8, 105 (ill.), 107, 113 (ill.)
walks on Moon, *A: 1:* 178; *B:* 4–6, 28–30
writes science fiction, *B:* 8–9

Aldrin, Edwin E. "Buzz," Jr., and Michael Collins, *PS:* **102–15**
excerpts from "The Eagle Has Landed," in *Apollo Expeditions to the Moon, PS:* 108–12

Alexander the Great
A: 1: 21–23

Alexandria, Egypt
A: 1: 23–24

Allen, Paul
A: 1: 151

Allies (Grand Alliance), in World War II
A: 1: 88, 93–94

ALMA. *See* Atacama Large Millimeter Array (ALMA)

Almagest (The Greatest; al-Majisti; He mathematike syntaxis; The Mathematical Compilation) (Ptolemy)
A: 1: 27, 30

Almaz military space station
A: 2: 214–16

Alpha Centauri, star nearest to Sun
A: 1: 6

Alpha Magnetic Spectrometer
B: 57

Alpha space station
B: 108

Alrai (star)
A: 1: 10

Altair (French-Russian mission to *Mir*)
B: 89

Altair (star)
A: 1: 9, 11

Amazing Stories
PS: 1

American astronauts

Aldrin, Buzz, *B:* 1–10
Apollo, *A: 1:* 171–98
Apollo 1 crew, *A: 1:* 172 (ill.); *B:* 11–21
Armstrong, Neil, *B:* 22–33
Bluford, Guy, *B:* 34–41
Challenger crew, *A: 1:* 175, 255–57, 256 (ill.); *B:* 42–50
Chang-Díaz, Franklin, *B:* 51–60
Collins, Eileen, *B:* 154
Columbia crew, *A: 2:* 266
Cooper, Gordon, *B:* 148 (ill.)
Cowings, Patricia, *B:* 119
Glenn, John, *B:* 69–78
Grissom, Gus, *B:* 148 (ill.)
Jarvis, Gregory, *B:* 43, 43 (ill.)
Jemison, Mae, *B:* 114–20
Lucid, Shannon, *B:* 136–45
McNair, Ronald, *B:* 42, 43 (ill.)
Mercury, *A: 1:* 140, 141
Mercury 7, *B:* 146–49, 148 (ill.)
Mercury 13, *B:* 146–55
on *Mir, A: 2:* 225
Ochoa, Ellen, *B:* 164–71
Onizuka, Ellison S., *B:* 42, 43 (ill.), 45
Resnick, Judith, *B:* 42, 43 (ill.)
Ride, Sally, *B:* 172–79
Schirra, Walter M., Jr., *B:* 148 (ill.)
Scobee, Francis, *B:* 42, 43 (ill.)
Shepard, Alan, *B:* 74, 74 (ill.), 148 (ill.)
Slayton, Donald "Deke," *B:* 148 (ill.)
Smith, Michael, *B:* 42, 43 (ill.)

American Civil War
A: 1: 56–57
PS: 3

American flag, on Moon
PS: 111–12, 113

American flight director, Kraft, Christopher
B: 128–35

American rocket pioneers
Goddard, Robert H., *B:* 79–86
von Braun, Wernher, *B:* 195–204

Ames Aeronautical Laboratory
A: 1: 125

AMU. *See* Astronaut Maneuvering Unit (AMU)

walks on Moon, *B:* 4–6,
28–30; *PS:* 107
Army Ballistic Missile Agency
(ABMA)
B: 161–62
Around the Moon (Verne)
A: 1: 62, 74
Around the World in Eighty Days
(Verne)
PS: 10
Artificial Earth, concept of. *See
also* Satellites
B: 192
Artificial satellite, defined
A: 1: 108, 130, 163; *2:* 190,
210, 304, 335
Artificial solar eclipse
A: 2: 201
Artillery experts
Congreve, William, *A: 1:* 55
Siemienowicz, Kazimierz, *A:
1:* 53–54
*Artis magnae artileria (Great Art
of Artillery)* (Siemienowicz)
A: 1: 53
Artwork, in Collier's series on
space travel
PS: 26
Artyukhin, Yuri
A: 2: 214
ASCA. *See* Advanced Satellite for
Cosmology and Astro-
physics (ASCA)
Asian American astronaut,
Onizuka, Ellison S.
B: 37
Asterism, *A: 1:* 7
defined, *A: 1:* 4
Asteroids
A: 2: 360–63
ASTP. *See* Apollo-Soyuz test
project
Astrology, defined
A: 1: 24
Astronaut Maneuvering Unit
(AMU)
A: 2: 221
Astronaut Science Colloquium
Program
B: 59
Astronaut Science Support Group
B: 59

Astronaut Training Base (Bei-
jing, China)
B: 216
Astronaut training program
(NASA), *B:* 3–4, 26–28. *See
also* Project Mercury
Mercury 7, *B:* 146–49; *PS:* 104
Mercury 13, *B:* 146–55, 147
(ill.)
opens to women and minorities, *B:* 34–35, 36–39
Astronautics, *A: 1:* 64, 128; *PS:*
41. *See also* Space travel
defined, *A: 1:* 130
Astronauts. *See also* American astronauts
effects of acceleration on, *A:
1:* 69
hero status of, *A: 1:* 133
safety of, in Project Mercury,
PS: 62–63
on space shuttle, *A: 2:* 238
and space stations, *PS:* 145
women, *PS:* 83 (ill.)
Astronomer(s), *A: 1:* 1–20
Aristarchus of Samos, *A:
1:* 26–27
Brahe, Tycho, *A: 1:* 35–37
Copernicus, Nicolaus, *A:
1:* 33–35, 34 (ill.)
Eratosthenes, *A: 1:* 27
Eudoxus of Cnidus, *A: 1:* 25
Galileo (Galileo Galilei), *A:
1:* 38–41, 40 (ill.)
Hipparchus, *A: 1:* 27–30
Kepler, Johannes, *A: 1:* 37
(ill.), 37–38
Astronomy, *A: 1:* 1–19, 21–43;
2: 301; *B:* 94, 96–97. *See
also* Astronomer(s); Ground-
based observatories; Hubble
Space Telescope (HST);
Space-based observatories;
Telescopes
ancient Greeks and, *A: 1:* 8–9,
25–31
Arabs and, *A: 1:* 8–9
defined, *A: 2:* 274, 304
infrared, *A: 2:* 292–93
as most ancient science, *A:
1:* 8–9
radio, *A: 2:* 287–92, 291 (ill.)
Sumerians and, *A: 1:* 8

Astounding Science Fiction
PS: 1
Astrophysicist, Spitzer, Lyman,
Jr.
A: 2: 308–9, 309 (ill.)
Asuka satellite observatory
A: 2: 328
AT&T Telstar satellite (United
States)
B: 139
Atacama Desert
A: 2: 299
Atacama Large Millimeter Array
(ALMA)
A: 2: 291–92
ATDA. *See* Augmented Target
Docking Adapter (ATDA)
Atkov, Oleg
A: 2: 217
Atlantis missions, *A: 2:* 252, 264,
354
Chang-Díaz, Franklin, *B:* 54–55
Lucid, Shannon, *B:* 139–40,
141–42, 143–44; *PS:* 148
Ochoa, Ellen, *B:* 168, 169
Atlantis space shuttle
PS: 130
Atlas-D launch vehicles
A: 1: 132
PS: 62, 66, 93
ATM. *See* Apollo Telescope
Mount (ATM)
"Atoms for Peace" (traveling sci-
ence exhibition)
B: 52–53
Atmosphere. *See* Earth's atmos-
phere
Atmospheric drag
A: 2: 247
Atmospheric Laboratory for Ap-
plications and Science
(ATLAS)
B: 168
Atmospheric phenomenon,
study of on space shuttle
B: 39
Atomic bomb, *A: 1:* 96 (ill.); *PS:*
1, 52
defined, *A: 1:* 88
first test, *A: 1:* 96–97
Manhattan Project, *A:
1:* 97–98
Auburn, Massachusetts
A: 1: 72

Augmented Target Docking Adapter (ATDA)
A: 1: 154–55
Aurora, *A: 1:* 113, 114
defined, *A: 1:* 108
Aurora 7
A: 1: 144–46
PS: 63
Authors
Aldrin, Buzz, *B:* 1–10, 9 (ill.)
Oberth, Hermann, *B:* 159–61
Ride, Sally, *B:* 177–78
Tsiolkovsky, Konstantin, *B:* 193–94
Wells, H. G., *B:* 205–13
Autogenic Feedback Training Exercise (AFTE)
B: 118, 119

B

Baade, Walter
A: 2: 297
Babylonians (ancient), astronomy of
A: 1: 28
Backsight
A: 2: 277
Bacon, Roger, and gunpowder recipe
A: 1: 50
Baikonur Cosmodrome
A: 1: 114–15
B: 126, 126 (ill.), 183
PS: 148
Baikonur Space Center
A: 2: 200
Bales, Steve
PS: 110
Ballistic missile, *A: 1:* 110. See also V-2 rocket
defined, *A: 1:* 108, 130
Jupiter, *A: 1:* 81
long-range, *A: 1:* 130–31
Korolev, Sergei, and, *PS:* 42, 46
Balloons, Tsiolkovsky and
B: 190–91
Bamboo tubes with gunpowder, as weapons
A: 1: 48
Barnes, John
B: 8

Basic rocket equation
A: 1: 66
B: 192
PS: 41
Bassett, Charles A., II
A: 1: 154
Battle of Bladensburg
A: 1: 55–56
Battle of Fort McHenry (Baltimore, Maryland)
A: 1: 45–47, 46 (ill.), 56
Battle of Leipzig (Battle of the Nations)
A: 1: 55
Bay of Pigs invasion (Cuba)
PS: 51
Bazooka
A: 1: 71
B: 83
PS: 13
Beagle 2 Mars lander
A: 2: 351
Bean, Alan L.
A: 1: 179; *2:* 220
Beggs, James M.
PS: 134
Bellifortis (War Fortifications) (von Eichstadt)
A: 1: 51
Belyayev, Pavel
A: 1: 149
Bends, *A: 2:* 200
defined, *A: 2:* 190
Beregovoi, Georgi T.
A: 1: 175
Berkner, Lloyd
A: 1: 113
Berlin Airlift
A: 1: 101
Beyond the Planet Earth (Tsiolkovsky)
A: 1: 69; *2:* 209
B: 193, 194
Big bang theory, *A: 2:* 313–14; *B:* 97; *PS:* 162–63, 164, 165 (ill.)
defined, *A: 2:* 274, 304
and radio astronomy, *A: 2:* 290, 303
Big Dipper
A: 1: 7
Big Three, *A: 1:* 94–95
defined, *A: 1:* 88

Binary star, defined
A: 2: 304
Biochemist, Lucid, Shannon
B: 136–45
BioSentient Corporation
B: 118
Biringuccio, Vannoccio
A: 1: 52–53
Black holes, *A: 2:* 317; *B:* 100; *PS:* 165
defined, *A: 2:* 304
Black powder. *See also* Gunpowder
A: 1: 48; *B:* 216
"Black Suits Comin', Nod Ya Head" (music video)
B: 40
Blaha, John
A: 2: 225
Blazars, gamma ray
A: 2: 321
Bluford, Guy, *B:* 34–41, 35 (ill.), 38 (ill.)
prejudice and, *B:* 36–39
Bolden, Charles F., Jr.
B: 99
Bolshevik Revolution
A: 1: 69, 87–90
Bolshevik(s). *See also* Communist Party
defined, *A: 1:* 88
Bomb. *See* Atomic bomb; Hydrogen bomb
"Bombs bursting in air"
A: 1: 45–47, 46 (ill.)
Bonestell, Chesley
PS: 26
Booster rockets, of space shuttle
A: 2: 243 (ill.), 243–44, 260–61; *PS:* 96–97, 129, 137
Borman, Frank
A: 1: 153, 176 (ill.), 176–77
B: 133–34
Borrelly comet
A: 2: 361
Boy Scout meets astronaut
B: 25
Brahe, Tycho
A: 1: 35–37
Braille (asteroid)
A: 2: 361
Brand, Vance
A: 2: 198–205, 199 (ill.)
Brandt, Willy
A: 2: 196

Brezhnev, Leonid
  A: 2: 201
  B: 185
"The Brick Moon: From the Papers of Captain Frederic Ingham" (Hale)
  A: 2: 209
  B: 106
  PS: 145–46
Briggs, Jane. *See* Hart, Janey
Brown, David M.
  A: 1: 175; *2:* 266
  PS: 178, 179 (ill.)
Brown dwarf, defined
  A: 2: 304
Burnell, Jocelyn Bell
  A: 2: 290
Bursts, gamma ray
  A: 2: 320
Bush, George H. W., *PS:*
  133–36, 136 (ill.)
  Remarks Announcing the
    Winner of the Teacher in
    Space Project, *PS:* 134–36
Bush, George W., *B:* 135; *PS:*
  58, 112–13, 185, **188–203,**
  193 (ill.)
  mourns *Columbia* crew, *PS:*
    126, 178, 199
  Remarks on a New Vision for
    Space Exploration Program,
    A: 2: 269, 318–19; *PS:* 131,
    157, 172, 192–99
Businesspeople
  Armstrong, Neil, *B:* 31–32
  Bluford, Guy, *B:* 40
  Glenn, John, *B:* 13, 69–78
  Jemison, Mae, *B:* 117–18
Buzz Lightyear
  B: 9
Bykovsky, Valery
  A: 1: 138
  B: 183, 184, 185 (ill.)

C

Cagle, Myrtle "K"
  B: 147 (ill.), 150
  PS: 77, 77 (ill.)
Calculus
  B: 158
Calendars

ancient Native American, *A:
    2:* 277
  and Hipparchus, *A: 1:* 29
  Stonehenge as, *A: 1:* 16 (ill.),
    17
Callisto (moon)
  A: 2: 356
Cameras
  on Hubble Space Telescope,
    B: 95–96, 100
  television, on Apollo flights,
    B: 134
Cameron, Kenneth D.
  B: 99
Canada
  A: 2: 232
Canadian Space Agency
  A: 2: 327
Canary Islands
  A: 2: 286
Cannon into space, in *From the
    Earth to the Moon* (Verne)
  PS: 3, 5–9, 8 (ill.)
Canon law
  A: 1: 32
Cape Canaveral, Florida
  A: 1: 167; *2:* 201, 244
Capitalism
  defined, *A: 1:* 88
  Marx, Karl, on, *A: 1:* 89–90
Capsule approach, to manned
    spaceflight
  PS: 66–67
Capsule communicator ("capcom")
  B: 174
Carbonate globules, in Mars meteorite
  PS: 160–61
Carbon-carbon tiles
  A: 2: 241
Cargo, before shuttles
  A: 2: 236
Cargo bay, of space shuttle
  A: 2: 241, 243 (ill.)
Carina (constellation)
  A: 1: 8, 14
Carpenter, M. Scott
  A: 1: 141, 144–46
  B: 148 (ill.), 149
  PS: 61, 61 (ill.), 63, 75
Carr, Gerald P.
  A: 2: 221

Cassini, Gian Domenico
  A: 2: 357
Cassini spacecraft
  PS: 171
Cassini-Huygens mission
  PS: 171
Cassini-Huygens spacecraft
  A: 2: 357
Cassiopeé mission
  B: 90–91
Cassiopeia (constellation)
  A: 1: 14, 36
Castro, Fidel
  PS: 51
Celestial bodies, movement of
  A: 1: 25 (ill.), 25–26, 38, 40,
    42–43
Celestial (Newtonian) mechanics
  A: 1: 24, 43
Celestial sphere, *A: 1:* 6
  defined, *A: 1:* 4, 24
  location of stars on, *A: 1:* 14
Centaurus (constellation)
  A: 1: 14
Cepheid variable stars
  A: 2: 274, 295, 297
Cepheus (constellation)
  A: 1: 10, 14
Ceremonial items, for Apollo-
    Soyuz test project
  A: 2: 202–3
Cernan, Eugene
  A: 1: 154, 155, 182
  PS: 196
Chaffee, Roger. *See also Apollo 1*
    crew
  A: 1: 171–73, 175
  B: 11, 12 (ill.), 17–19, 18 (ill.),
    133
  PS: 72, 104
Chagas's disease
  B: 58
Chaika (Seagull)
  B: 183
Challenger, A: 2: 252; *PS:* 130,
  136–44. *See also* Space
    shuttles
  Address to the Nation on the
    Explosion of the Space
    Shuttle (Reagan), *PS:*
    139–41
  Bluford, Guy and, *B:* 39

Democracy, *A: 1:* 90
  defined, *A: 1:* 88–89
Deneb (star)
  A: 1: 9, 11
Depression, and Aldrin, Buzz
  B: 8
Descartes Highlands
  A: 1: 182
Destiny control module, of International Space Station
  A: 2: 233
Destiny laboratory (U.S. ISS module)
  B: 111
Détente
  A: 2: 190, 194–96
Dialogo Galilei linceo . . . sopra i due massimi sistemi del mondo (Dialogue on the Two Chief Systems of the World) (Galileo)
  A: 1: 40
Dialogue on the Two Chief Systems of the World (Dialogo Galilei linceo . . . sopra i due massimi sistemi del mondo) (Galileo)
  A: 1: 40
Die Rakete zu den Planeträumen (The Rocket into Planetary Space) (Oberth)
  A: 1: 75; *2:* 210
  B: 159–60
Dietrich, Jan
  B: 150
  PS: 77
Dietrich, Marion
  B: 150–51
  PS: 77
Dirigible
  B: 191
Discoverer 14
  A: 1: 125
Discovery missions, *A: 2:* 252, 262, 264, 317; *B:* 55 (ill.); *PS:* 129
  Bluford, Guy, *B:* 39
  Chang-Díaz, Franklin, *B:* 54–55, 57
  Glenn, John, *B:* 76, 77; *PS:* 91–92, 96–99
  Hubble Space Telescope, *B:* 99

Lucid, Shannon, *B:* 139
Ochoa, Ellen, *B:* 168–69
  and Spacelab-J, *B:* 116–17
Discrimination, against women in space program
  PS: 86–87
Disney, Walt
  A: 1: 110; *2:* 211
DM. *See* Docking Module (Apollo-Soyuz)
Dobrovolsky, Georgy
  A: 1: 175; *2:* 192, 213
Docking module (Apollo-Soyuz)
  A: 2: 188 (ill.), 198–200
Docking system, defined
  A: 2: 190
"Dog days of summer"
  A: 1: 11–13
Dog in space
  B: 64, 64 (ill.)
  PS: 46
Dog Star (Sirius)
  A: 1: 6, 11–13
Dollard, John
  A: 2: 283
Dominance in space. *See also* Cold War
  B: 13
Dornberger, Walter
  B: 199
  PS: 26
Draco (constellation)
  A: 1: 10, 14
Drake, Francis
  PS: 140–41
Drayton, Ken
  B: 25
"Dreams of the Earth and Sky and the Effects of Universal Gravitation" (Tsiolkovsky)
  A: 1: 65–66
  B: 192
Dryden, Hugh L.
  A: 1: 126 (ill.)
Duke, Charles M., Jr.
  A: 1: 182
  PS: 110
Dwarf galaxies
  A: 2: 293
Dynasoar (experimental spacecraft)
  B: 26

E

EAC. *See* European Astronaut Corps (EAC)
EADS Phoenix space shuttle
  A: 2: 267
"The Eagle Has Landed" (Collins and Aldrin)
  PS: 102–15
Eagle lunar landing module, *A: 1:* 178; *B:* 2, 28, 29 (ill.), 30; *PS:* 54 (ill.), 103, 105–7
  for *Apollo 11*, *B:* 4
Earth. *See also* the Origins Initiative; Precession
  ancient Greeks and, *A: 1:* 25–31
  artificial, concept of, *B:* 192
  axis of, *A: 1:* 9–10, 28
  circumference of, *A: 1:* 27
  distance from Moon, *A: 1:* 29
  distance from Sun, *A: 1:* 5–6
  in early astronomy, *B:* 96–97
  magnetic field, *A: 1:* 120
  movement through space, *A: 1:* 9–14
  orbit around Sun, *A: 1:* 11
  origins of life on, *PS:* 164
  returning to, in Project Mercury, *PS:* 62–63
  shape of, *A: 1:* 9
  shuttle orbit of, *A: 2:* 247
  from space, *A: 1:* 177; *2:* 233; *PS:* 95, 99, 197 (ill.)
Earth from space
  Armstrong, Neil, on, *B:* 32
  Gagarin, Yuri, on, *B:* 65
  Ochoa, Ellen, *B:* 168
  returning to, *B:* 13, 183–84
  Yang Liwei, *B:* 217
Earth-centered model of planetary motion. *See* Geocentric (Earth-centered) model of planetary motion
EarthKAM
  B: 177
"Earthrise" (photograph)
  A: 1: 177
Earth's atmosphere
  filters cosmic radiation, *A: 2:* 276
  limits telescopes, *A: 2:* 276, 286, 287; *B:* 97–98
  ozone layer, *A: 2:* 306

Exercise, on *Skylab*
  A: 2: 218, 221
Exhaust velocity, defined
  A: 1: 48
Expedition-8 (ISS)
  PS: 191
Experimental aircraft and space-
  craft
  Armstrong, Neil, *B:* 24–26
  Goddard, Robert H., *A: 1:* 73;
    B: 85
  Oberth, Hermann, *B:*
    161–62
  Tsiolkovsky, Konstantin, *B:*
    190–93; *PS:* 40–41
Experimental method, modern,
  Galileo (Galileo Galilei)
  A: 1: 39
Experiments. *See also* individual
  astronauts and shuttle mis-
  sions
  exploring origins of life and
    space, *PS:* 163–65
  on *Friendship 7, B:* 72
  Lunar Laser Ranging Experi-
    ment, *B:* 31
  on *Mir, B:* 143; *PS:* 149,
    152–53, 157
  on Moon, *A: 1:* 182
  and Project Gemini, *A: 1:*
    153
  and Project Mercury, *PS:*
    70–71
  on reaching extreme altitudes
    (Goddard), *PS:* 14–19
  on *Skylab, A: 2:* 220–21
  on space shuttle, *A: 2:* 264,
    265; *PS:* 122
  on space stations, *A: 2:* 209,
    233–35
  on Spacelab, *A: 2:* 253 (ill.),
    254
Exploration
  ages of, *A: 1:* 59–61
  literature and, *A: 1:* 61–63
"Exploration of the Universe
  with Reaction Machines"
  (Tsiolkovsky)
  A: 1: 66
Explorer 1 satellite
  A: 1: 81, 114, 122–24, 123
    (ill.), 132
  B: 201
  PS: 37

Exploring Our Solar System (Ride)
  B: 178
*Exploring the Unknown: Selected
  Documents in the History of
  the U.S. Civil Space Program,
  Volume 1: Organizing for Ex-
  ploration*
  PS: 116, 160
Explosive weapons
  A: 1: 48
External fuel tank, of space
  shuttle
  A: 2: 242–43, 243 (ill.), 244,
    246
Extravehicular activities (EVAs)
  (spacewalks), *A: 1:* 148,
    152, 156, 157–58, 182. *See
    also* Spacewalks
  Cernan, Eugene, *A: 1:* 155
  and International Space Sta-
    tion, *B:* 109
  untethered, *A: 2:* 254
  White, Edward, *B:* 17
Extreme Ultraviolet Explorer
  (EUVE)
  A: 2: 312
Extremely High Frequency (EHF)
  range
  A: 2: 289
Eye, in stargazing
  A: 2: 277
Eyeglasses
  A: 2: 278
Eyepiece, of telescope
  A: 2: 282

F

Fabian, John M.
  B: 174
FAI. *See* International Aeronauti-
  cal Foundation (FAI)
Faint-object camera, on Hubble
  Space Telescope
  B: 95, 96
Faint-object spectrograph, on
  Hubble Space Telescope
  B: 95, 96
Faith 7
  A: 1: 146
  PS: 64

Far Infrared and Submillimeter
  Telescope (Herschel Tele-
  scope)
  A: 2: 329
Far Ultraviolet Spectroscopic Ex-
  plorer (FUSE)
  A: 2: 312–13
Farming societies, and regular
  observation of sky
  A: 1: 15–16
Fast solar wind
  A: 2: 364
"Father of astronautics." *See* Tsi-
  olkovsky, Konstantin
F8U Crusader
  B: 71
  PS: 90
Female astronauts. *See* Women
  astronauts
Feoktistov, Konstantin
  A: 1: 149
Fighter pilots
  Aldrin, Buzz, *B:* 3
  Armstrong, Neil, *B:* 24
  Bluford, Guy, *B:* 36
  Glenn, John, *B:* 71
Filipchenko, Anatoli V.
  A: 1: 179
Fincke, Edward Michael
  PS: 157, 200
*Find Where the Wind Goes: Mo-
  ments from My Life* (Jemi-
  son)
  B: 118
Fire arrows, as first rockets
  A: 1: 49 (ill.), 49–50
Fire, in cockpit of *Apollo/Saturn
  204*
  B: 19–20
Fire pots, as weapons
  A: 1: 48
Firecrackers
  A: 1: 48
"Fireflies"
  A: 1: 145–46
Fireworks, *A: 1:* 48
  components of, *A: 1:* 49
First satellite, *PS:* **40–49**, 41
    (ill.), 45 (ill.), 74
  "Announcement of the First
    Satellite" (originally pub-
    lished in *Pravda*), *PS:* 43–45

From the Earth to the Moon: Passage Direct in Ninety-seven Hours and Twenty Minutes (Verne)
A: 1: 62, 74, 107 (ill.)
B: 159
PS: 5–9, 6 (ill.), 8 (ill.)
Fronsperger, Leonhart
A: 1: 51
Fuel for moon ship, von Braun, Wernher, envisions
PS: 32
Fuel, rocket
PS: 14
Fuel tank (external), of space shuttle
A: 2: 242–43, 243 (ill.), 244, 246
PS: 98, 129
Fullerton, C. Gordon
A: 2: 251
Funk, Wally
B: 147 (ill.), 151, 152, 154
PS: 77, 77 (ill.), 88
FUSE. *See* Far Ultraviolet Spectroscopic Explorer (FUSE)
Fusion, nuclear, *A: 1:* 99
defined, *A: 1:* 4

G

Gagarin, Yuri, *A: 1:* 135–37, 136 (ill.); *B:* **61–68,** 62 (ill.)
awards, *B:* 66–67
dies in training crash, *A: 1:* 175–76; *B:* 67
early life, *B:* 61–63
hailed as hero, *B:* 65–66
pioneers human space flight, *A: 1:* 135–36, 162; *2:* 189; *B:* 12–13, 63–65, 121, 131, 153, 180; *PS:* 46, 51, 92, 116, 189
prepares for aviation career, *B:* 63
Galaxies, *A: 1:* 1–8; *2:* 293; *B:* 97
Andromeda, *A: 1:* 6; *2:* 285, 295
defined, *A: 1:* 4; *2:* 274
Hubble Deep Field, *A: 2:* 317
Hubble's study of, *A: 2:* 295, 313

Milky Way, *A: 1:* 1–2
redshift of, *A: 2:* 295–96
Galilean moons
A: 1: 39–40
Galileo (Galileo Galilei)
A: 1: 38–41, 40 (ill.), 182; *2:* 279–83, 281 (ill.)
B: 97
Galileo spacecraft
A: 2: 264, 334, 353
B: 54, 139
Gamma Cephi (star)
A: 1: 10
Gamma ray blazers
A: 2: 321
Gamma ray bursts
A: 2: 320
Gamma Ray Large Area Telescope (GLAST)
A: 2: 329
Gamma rays, *A: 2:* 273, 306 (ill.), 307; *B:* 100; *PS:* 165
defined, *A: 1:* 108; *2:* 274, 304
Ganymede (moon)
A: 2: 356
Garn, Jake
A: 2: 254
Garriot, Owen K.
A: 2: 220
GAS payloads (Small Self-Contained Payloads, or Getaway Specials)
B: 139
Gases, kinetic theory of
A: 1: 64
Gauss, Carl Friedrich
A: 1: 111
Gehman, Harold W., Jr.
A: 2: 267–70
Gellius, Aulus
A: 1: 47
Gemini (Molly Brown)
B: 16
Gemini North Telescope
A: 2: 297
Gemini Project. *See* Project Gemini
Gemini spacecraft program, *A: 1:* 150–58
dimensions of, *A: 1:* 150
Gemini 3, *A: 1:* 151
Gemini 4, *A: 1:* 152; *B:* 6–17
Gemini 5, *A: 1:* 152–53

Gemini 6, *A: 1:* 153
Gemini 7, *A: 1:* 153–54
Gemini 8, *A: 1:* 154; *B:* 7 (ill.); *PS:* 104
Gemini 9, *A: 1:* 154–55
Gemini 10, *A: 1:* 155; *PS:* 104
Gemini 11, *A: 1:* 155–56
Gemini 12, *A: 1:* 157–58; *B:* 3; *PS:* 104
Geocentric (Earth-centered) model of planetary motion
Aristotle, *A: 1:* 25 (ill.), 25–26
Brahe, Tycho, *A: 1:* 36–37
defined, *A: 1:* 24
Ptolemy, *A: 1:* 29–33
Geophysics
A: 1: 113
George C. Marshall Space Flight Center
A: 1: 82
B: 202
PS: 37
Geosynchronous orbit, *A: 2:* 310
defined, *A: 2:* 304
German Army Ordnance Office rocket program
B: 198
German Rocket Society (Verein für Raumschiffahrt)
B: 160, 197
German scientists, *A: 1:* 130
Oberth, Hermann, *A: 1:* 74–79, 75 (ill.); *B:* 156–63, 197
von Braun, Wernher, *B:* 79, 161, 195–204; *PS:* 24–26, 38
Germany
and development of V-2 rocket, *A: 1:* 130; *B:* 124
divided after World War II, *A: 1:* 101
early military rockets, *A: 1:* 51, 73
World War II, *A: 1:* 73, 93, 95; *B:* 160–61, 197–99
Gernsback, Hugo
PS: 10
Getaway Specials (Small Self-Contained Payloads, or GAS payloads)
B: 139
Gibson, Edward G.
A: 2: 221

Gibson, Robert "Hoot"
  B: 141
Gidzenko, Yuri
  A: 2: 234
  B: 110
Giotto space probe
  A: 2: 361
GIRD. *See* Group for Investigation of Reactive Motion (GIRD)
GIRD-9 and GIRD-10
  B: 123, 124
Glassmaking, and lenses
  A: 2: 278
GLAST. *See* Gamma Ray Large Area Telescope (GLAST)
Glenn, John, *A: 1:* 141, 144; *B:* 13, **69–78,** 70 (ill.), 73 (ill.), 148 (ill.), 149; *PS:* 56, 61, 61 (ill.), 63, 75, 91 (ill.), 94 (ill.), 97 (ill.), 102, 189
  orbits Earth, *B:* 71–73, 132
  tests space travel for older people, *B:* 76–77; *PS:* 91–92, 97 (ill.), 99
Glenn, John, with Nick Taylor,
  PS: **90–101**
  excerpts from *John Glenn: A Memoir, PS:* 93–99
Glennan, T. Keith
  A: 1: 125–27, 126 (ill.)
  B: 148
  PS: 75, 79
Glider, space shuttle as
  A: 2: 251
Gliders, Korolev, Sergei and
  B: 123
  PS: 41
Glushko, Valentin Petrovich
  B: 123, 126
  PS: 42
"Go-Cycler"
  B: 8
Goddard, Robert H., *A:* 1: 69–74, 70 (ill.); *B:* **79–86,** 80 (ill.), 84 (ill.); *PS:* **12–23,** 13 (ill.), 18 (ill.), 41–42
  excerpt from *A Method of Reaching Extreme Altitudes* (Goddard), *PS:* 14–19
  invents two-stage rocket, *B:* 82–83, 124
Goddard Space Flight Center
  A: 1: 74, 126

Gods, of sky
  A: 1: 15
Godwin, Linda
  A: 2: 227 (ill.)
Golf, on the Moon
  A: 1: 181
Gorbatko, Viktor V.
  A: 1: 179
Gordon, Richard F., Jr.
  A: 1: 155–56, 179
Gore, Al
  PS: 162
Gorelick, Sarah Lee. *See* Ratley, Sarah
Grand Alliance (Allies), in World War II
  A: 1: 93–94
"The Graphical Depiction of Sensations" (Tsiolkovsky)
  B: 190
Gravitation, universal, Newton's law of
  A: 1: 42
Gravity. *See also* Precession
  acceleration and, *B:* 191
  defined, *A: 1:* 24
  forces exerted on Earth by Sun and Moon, *A: 1:* 28, 29 (ill.)
  on Moon, *B:* 6
  and Newton, Isaac, *A: 1:* 41–43
  reduced, effect on humans, *A: 2:* 233
Gravity assist
  A: 2: 346
Great Art of Artillery (Artis magnae artileria) (Siemienowicz)
  A: 1: 53
Great Britain, and World War II
  A: 1: 93–94
Great Dark Spot (Neptune)
  A: 2: 360
Great Depression
  A: 1: 92
Great Observatories (NASA)
  A: 2: 264, 302 (ill.), 315
Great Square of Pegasus (constellation)
  A: 1: 11
Great Wall of China
  B: 218–19
Great Work (Opus Majus) (Bacon)
  A: 1: 50

The Greatest (Almagest; al-Majisti; He mathematike syntaxis; The Mathematical Compilation) (Ptolemy)
  A: 1: 30
Grechko, Georgi
  A: 2: 214–16
Greeks (ancient)
  and constellations, *A: 1:* 8–9
  and "dog days of summer," *A: 1:* 11–13
  form foundation of modern astronomy, *A: 1:* 21–31
  and Renaissance, *A: 1:* 33
Grissom, Gus, *A: 1:* 141, 143–44, 173; *B:* 11, 12 (ill.), 15 (ill.), 15–16, 72, 133, 148 (ill.), 149; *PS:* 61 (ill.), 62, 63, 72, 75, 104. *See also* *Apollo 1* crew
  dies in *Apollo/Saturn 204* spacecraft fire, *A: 1:* 171–73, 175
  Gemini 3 flight, *A: 1:* 151, 163
  Liberty Bell 7 flight, *PS:* 63
Ground-based observatories, *A: 1:* 15–19; 2: 271–300
  ancient, *A: 2:* 276–77
  best sites for, *A: 2:* 286–87
  cost of, *A: 2:* 276
  early telescopes as, *A: 2:* 278–85
  giant, *A: 2:* 297–99
  Hubble, Edwin, and, *A: 2:* 294–97
  infrared astronomy at, *A: 2:* 292–93
  modern telescopes in, *A: 2:* 285–87
  optical astronomy at, *A: 2:* 293–99
  radio astronomy at, *A: 2:* 287–92
Group for Investigation of Reactive Motion (GIRD)
  B: 123, 124
  PS: 41
Grover's Mills, New Jersey
  A: 1: 100
Gubarev, Aleksei
  A: 2: 214–16
Guggenheim, Daniel
  B: 84

Guggenheim Fund for the Promotion of Aeronautics
A: 1: 72
Guidance system (rocket), development of
B: 84–85
Gunpowder
Chinese and, A: 1: 48–50
defined, A: 1: 48
Europeans and, A: 1: 50–55
Guth, Alan
A: 2: 314
Gyroscopes
A: 1: 73; 2: 315–16

H

Haas, Conrad, multistage rocket
A: 1: 52
Haigneré, Claudie
B: 87–93, 88 (ill.), 92 (ill.)
Haigneré, Jean-Pierre, B: 89, 90, 90 (ill.), 92 (ill.)
and Mir, B: 90, 90 (ill.), 107–8; PS: 157
Haise, Fred W., Jr.
A: 1: 180–81; 2: 251
PS: 112
HALCA. See Highly Advanced Laboratory for Communications and Astronomy (HALCA)
Hale, Edward Everett
A: 2: 209
B: 106
PS: 145–46
Hale, George
A: 2: 294
Hale rockets
A: 1: 56–57
Hale Telescope (Palomar)
A: 2: 272 (ill.)
Hale, William
A: 1: 56–57
Hall, Chester Moor
A: 2: 283
Halley, Edmond
A: 1: 42; 2: 361
Halley's comet
A: 2: 361

Halley's comet, and Spartan-Halley comet research observatory
B: 47
Ham (chimpanzee in space)
A: 1: 143
PS: 63, 69 (ill.)
Handgun, first
A: 1: 51
"Handshake in space." See Apollo-Soyuz test project
Hard landing, defined
A: 2: 335
Harriot, Thomas
A: 2: 279
Hart, Janey, A: 1: 140; B: 151, 152–53; PS: 77, 78
meets with President Johnson, PS: 83–86
Haruka satellite observatory
A: 2: 328
Hawley, Steven A.
B: 99
H-bomb. See Hydrogen bomb
He mathematike syntaxis (The Mathematical Compilation; al-Majisti; Almagest; The Greatest) (Ptolemy)
A: 1: 30
HEAO. See High Energy Astrophysical Observatories (HEAO)
Heat shield incident, Friendship 7
B: 72–74, 132
PS: 91
Heavy Row
PS: 96
Heel Stone (Stonehenge)
A: 1: 17
Heliocentric (Sun-centered) model of planetary motion, A: 1: 26–27
Brahe, Tycho, A: 1: 36–37
Copernicus, Nicholas, A: 1: 33–35
defined, A: 1: 24
Galileo, A: 1: 40–41
Heliosphere, A: 2: 364
defined, A: 2: 335
Hellenism (Greek culture)
defined, A: 1: 24
science and, A: 1: 24–25
spread of, A: 1: 23

Heresy, of Galileo
A: 1: 40–41
Hero (Heron) of Alexandria
A: 1: 47
Hero status, of astronauts
A: 1: 133
Hero's engine (aeolipile)
A: 1: 47
Herrington, John Bennett
B: 37
Herschel Telescope
A: 2: 329
Herschel, William
A: 2: 284, 358
Hewish, Antony
A: 2: 290
High altitudes, for ground-based observatory
A: 2: 287
High Energy Astrophysical Observatories (HEAO)
A: 2: 319, 321
Highly Advanced Laboratory for Communications and Astronomy (HALCA)
A: 2: 328
High-resolution spectrograph, on Hubble Space Telescope
B: 95, 96
High-speed photometer, on Hubble Space Telescope
B: 95
Himmler, Heinrich
B: 199
PS: 26
Hipparchus
A: 1: 27–30
Hiroshima, Japan
A: 1: 97
Hispanic American astronaut, Ochoa, Ellen
B: 164–71
Histoire comique des états et empires de la lune (Comical History of the States and Empires of the Moon) (Cyrano de Bergerac)
A: 1: 61
The History of Mr. Polly (Wells)
B: 210
Hitler, Adolf
A: 1: 79, 93
B: 197
PS: 26

Hixon, Jean
  B: 151
  PS: 77
Ho Chi Minh
  A: 2: 195
Hobby-Eberly Telescope
  A: 2: 298
Hooker, John D.
  A: 2: 294
Hooker telescope
  A: 2: 294
Horizon marks, in ancient observatories
  A: 2: 277
Hornet (aircraft carrier)
  B: 6, 30
A House in the Sky (Cooper)
  PS: 153
House Un-American Activities
  Committee
  A: 1: 102
Houston, Texas
  A: 1: 152
HST. *See* Hubble Space Telescope
  (HST)
Hsue-Shen, Tsien
  B: 216
Hubble, Edwin P.
  A: 2: 294–97, 313
  B: 94, 97, 98
Hubble Space Telescope (HST),
  A: 2: 264, 302 (ill.), 315–19;
  B: 94–103, 95 (ill.); *PS:* 170,
  190
  Columbia and, *PS:* 181
  future of, *PS:* 170, 199–200
  history of, *B:* 97–99
  repair missions to, *A:
    2:* 316–18; *B:* 99–100
  workings of, *B:* 95–96
Hubble Ultra Deep Field
  A: 2: 316
Hubble's law
  A: 2: 295–96
Hundred Years War
  A: 1: 51, 52 (ill.)
Huntress, Wesley
  PS: 163
Huntsville, Alabama
  A: 1: 78, 126; *2:* 211
  B: 161–62, 201
  PS: 37
Hurricane Mitch
  PS: 98

Husband, Rick D.
  A: 1: 175; *2:* 266
  PS: 178, 179 (ill.)
Huxley, Aldous
  PS: 10
Huxley, Thomas
  B: 207
Huygens, Christiaan
  A: 2: 356
Hyakutake comet
  A: 2: 312
Hyder Ali (Haider Ali), first
  metal-body rocket
  A: 1: 54–55
Hydra (constellation)
  A: 1: 8
Hydrocarbon
  defined, *A: 1:* 48
  liquid, *A: 1:* 67
Hydrogen bomb, *A: 1:* 99–100
  defined, *A: 1:* 88–89
  United States, *A: 1:* 99
Hydrogen, liquid
  A: 1: 67; *2:* 242
Hyperbaric chamber, *A:
  2:* 199–200
  defined, *A: 2:* 190
Hypersonic flight
  A: 1: 166

I

IAU. *See* International Astronomical Union (IAU)
ICBM. *See* Intercontinental Ballistic Missile (ICBM)
Ice, search for on Moon
  A: 2: 340–41
ICSU. *See* International Council
  of Scientific Unions (ICSU)
IGY. *See* International Geophysical Year (IGY)
Imaginary Lines
  B: 177
Inca
  A: 2: 277
India, Haider Ali (Hyder Ali)
  A: 1: 54–55
Inflationary theory (cosmology)
  A: 2: 304, 314
Infrared astronomy
  A: 2: 292–93, 326

Infrared radiation, *A: 2:* 273–76,
  306, 306 (ill.), 324
  defined, *A: 2:* 274, 304
  far, *A: 2:* 312–13, 329
Infrared Space Observatory (ISO)
  A: 2: 326
Infrared telescopes
  A: 2: 292–93
Inquisition
  A: 1: 40–41
Instruments, in scientific observation
  A: 2: 278
Insulating foam
  B: 44, 111–12
Insulating thermal tiles, of space
  shuttle
  A: 2: 241–42, 250–51
Insulation (foam), on *Columbia*
  A: 2: 268
  PS: 178–80, 181, 183, 190
Intercontinental Ballistic Missile
  (ICBM), *A: 1:* 98, 98 (ill.);
  B: 125
  Atlas, *A: 1:* 132
  Soviet, *A: 1:* 114–15
Interferometers, *A: 2:* 292, 298
  defined, *A: 2:* 274
International Aeronautical Foundation (FAI)
  A: 1: 137; *2:* 203
International Astronomical
  Union (IAU)
  A: 1: 8
International communications
  satellites
  B: 139, 174
International Council of Scientific Unions (ICSU)
  A: 1: 113
International Geophysical Year
  (IGY)
  A: 1: 111–14; *2:* 187
International Geophysical Year,
  and *Sputnik*
  PS: 44–45
International participation, in
  spaceflight
  PS: 123
International Polar Year (IPY)
  A: 1: 112–13
International Science Camp,
  Jemison, Mae
  B: 118

International Space Station (ISS), *A: 2:* 229–35, 230 (ill.), 232 (ill.); *B:* 44, 54, **104–13**, 105 (ill.), 110 (ill.), 134, 169; *PS:* 83 (ill.), 145, 190–91
  assembly phases, *B:* 108–11; *PS:* 202
  Columbia tragedy causes delay, *PS:* 156–57
  components of, *A: 2:* 232–33
  Destiny laboratory module, *A: 2:* 229–35
  dimensions, *A: 2:* 231
  experiments on, *A: 2:* 233–35
  largest international partnership in history, *B:* 104
  main components, *B:* 109
  space shuttle and, *A: 2:* 265
  U.S. goals for, *PS:* 195
  working on, *PS:* 200
  Zarya control module, *A: 2:* 233
  Zvezda service module, *A: 2:* 233
International Ultraviolet Explorer (IUE) *A: 2:* 310–12
Interorbital Systems *B:* 154; *PS:* 88
Interplanetary, defined *A: 2:* 335
Interplanetary medium, defined *A: 2:* 239
Interplanetary spacecraft. *See* Space probes
Interstellar, defined *A: 1:* 108; *2:* 304
Interstellar medium, *A: 2:* 310
  defined, *A: 2:* 304
Inventors, Hale, William *A: 1:* 56–57
"Investigations of Outer Space by Reaction Devices" (Tsiolkovsky) *B:* 193
The Invisible Man: A Grotesque Romance (Wells) *B:* 206, 210
Io (moon) *A: 2:* 355 (ill.)
Ionosphere, *A: 1:* 114
  defined, *A: 1:* 108

IPY. *See* International Polar Year (IPY)
Irwin, James B. *A: 1:* 181
The Island of Doctor Moreau: A Possibility (Wells) *B:* 206, 208–9
ISO. *See* Infrared Space Observatory (ISO)
Israel, Ramon, Ilan *A: 2:* 266
ISS. *See* International Space Station (ISS)
Italy, early military rockets *A: 1:* 51
Italy, Leonardo module (ISS component) *B:* 111
IUE. *See* International Ultraviolet Explorer (IUE)

J

James Webb Space Telescope *A: 2:* 316, 328
Jansky, Karl *A: 2:* 289–90
Japan
  Halley's comet probe, *A: 2:* 361
  Mars probe, *A: 2:* 350
  small space-based observatories, *A: 2:* 328
  and Spacelab-J, *B:* 116–17
  and World War II, *A: 1:* 93, 97–98
Japan Aerospace Exploration Agency (JAXA) *A: 2:* 350
Jarvis, Gregory *A: 1:* 175; *2:* 255, 256 (ill.); *B:* 43, 43 (ill.), 46; *PS:* 139
JAXA. *See* Japan Aerospace Exploration Agency (JAXA)
The Jemison Group *B:* 117–18
The Jemison Institute for Advancing Technology in Developing Countries *B:* 118
Jemison, Mae, *B:* 37, **114–20**, 115 (ill.), 117 (ill.)

  promotes science education, *B:* 118–20
  starts her own companies, *B:* 117–18
Jessen, Gene Nora *B:* 147 (ill.), 151; *PS:* 77, 77 (ill.)
Jesus of Nazareth *A: 1:* 32
Jet planes, and aircraft carriers *PS:* 21
Jet Propulsion Laboratory, and Lucid, Shannon *B:* 144
Jet-assisted takeoff (JATO) device *A: 1:* 73
Jettison, defined *A: 1:* 163
Jiuquan Launch Center (China) *B:* 216
Joan of Arc *A: 1:* 51, 52 (ill.)
"Joe-1" *A: 1:* 99
John Glenn: A Memoir (Glenn, with Taylor) *PS:* 90–101
John Paul II, Pope *A: 1:* 41
Johnson, Lyndon B., meets with Cobb and Hart *B:* 152–53; *PS:* 78, 83–86
Johnson Space Center *A: 1:* 152
Jornada del muerto (Journey of the Dead) *A: 1:* 96 (ill.), 97
Journey to the Center of the Earth (Verne) *A: 1:* 61–62; *PS:* 2
Junk, in space *A: 2:* 236, 360
Juno 1 launch vehicle *A: 1:* 81, 122
Jupiter, *A: 2:* 264, 290, 353–56
  moons of, *A: 1:* 39–40; *2:* 281, 355–56
  and Shoemaker-Levy 9 comet, *A: 2:* 317, 341
Jupiter C rocket *A: 1:* 81, 82 (ill.); *B:* 201

K

Kaleri, Alexander
  PS: 192
Kaluga, Russia
  A: 1: 63
  B: 190, 194
"Kaputnik"
  A: 1: 120
Kazakhstan
  A: 1: 99, 114
Keck Telescopes
  A: 2: 297–98, 298 (ill.)
Kennedy, John F., *A: 1:* 137,
  145 (ill.), 164 (ill.); *2:* 195;
  B: 131 (ill.), 131–32; *PS:*
  50–59, 51 (ill.), 64, 117,
  126, 189
  excerpt from Special Message
    to the Congress on Urgent
    National Needs, *PS:* 52–55
  and John Glenn, *B:* 75
  speech at Rice University, *PS:*
    58
  vows to put man on the
    moon, *A: 1:* 160, 162;
    2: 211; *B:* 11–12, 22, 107;
    PS: 58
Kennedy Space Center
  A: 1: 167; *2:* 201, 244, 247
Kepler, Johannes
  A: 1: 37 (ill.), 37–38, 43;
    2: 282
Kerwin, Joseph P.
  A: 2: 220
Key, Francis Scott
  A: 1: 45–47, 46 (ill.), 56
Khrunov, Yevgeny
  A: 1: 177
Khrushchev, Nikita
  A: 1: 119, 119 (ill.), 120, 135,
    147
  B: 66, 126, 183, 185 (ill.), 202
Kincheloe, Iven
  PS: 70
Kipps (Wells)
  B: 210
Kissinger, Henry A.
  A: 2: 196
Kizim, Leonid
  A: 2: 217
Klep, Rolf
  PS: 26
Klimuk, Pyotr
  A: 2: 215

Komarov, Vladimir
  A: 1: 149, 174, 175
  B: 67
Kondakova, Yelena
    Vladimirovna
  B: 144
Kopernik, Nicolause. *See* Copernicus, Nicolaus
Korda, Alexander
  B: 212
Korean War
  Aldrin, Buzz, *B:* 3
  Armstrong, Neil, *B:* 24
  Glenn, John, *B:* 71; *PS:* 90
Korolev, Sergei, *A: 1:* 116, 119,
  165; *B:* 65, **121–27,** 122
  (ill.); *PS:* 41–42
  development of rocket technology, *PS:* 41–42, 103
  develops R-7 rocket, *B:*
    124–25
  sent to prison, *B:* 123–24;
    PS: 47
Kosygin, Alexei
  A: 2: 196–97
Kraft, Christopher, *B:* **128–35,**
  129 (ill.)
  directs Mercury flights, *B:*
    130–32
  helps land men on Moon,
    B: 133–34
  recalls Glenn flight, *B:* 132–33
Krikalev, Sergei
  A: 2: 234
  B: 110
Kristall module
  A: 2: 224–25
Kubasov, Valeri
  A: 1: 179; *2:* 198, 199 (ill.)
Kummersdorf, Germany
  A: 1: 79
Kvant 1 module, of *Mir*
  A: 2: 224
Kvant 2 module, of *Mir*
  A: 2: 224

L

Lacaille, Nicolas Louis de
  A: 1: 8
Laika (first animal in space)
  A: 1: 117
  B: 64, 64 (ill.)
  PS: 46

Landing, hard, defined
  A: 2: 335
Landing, soft, defined
  A: 2: 335
Lang, Fritz
  A: 1: 76
  B: 160
Langley Aeronautical Laboratory
  A: 1: 125
Languages, in Apollo-Soyuz test
    project
  A: 2: 198
Large Space Telescope (LST) project
  A: 2: 315
  B: 98–99
  PS: 72, 112, 117–18, 189–90
Latina American astronaut,
    Ochoa, Ellen
  B: 37
Latino astronauts
  Chang-Díaz, Franklin, *B:* 51–60
  Neri Vela, Rodolfo, *B:* 37, 166
Law(s) of motion
  Newton, Isaac, *A: 1:* 42–43, 53
  third, *A: 1:* 66–67
Lawrence, Robert Henry Jr.
  B: 37, 39
Laws of planetary motion, Kepler, Johannes
  A: 1: 37–38
*Leadership and America's Future
    in Space* (Ride)
  B: 175–76
Lead-gold alloy, for Apollo-
    Soyuz test project
  A: 2: 203
Lebedev, Vladimir
  B: 67
Lenin, Vladimir I.
  A: 1: 89–90, 90 (ill.), 130
Lens(es), *A: 2:* 278–79
  achromatic, *A: 2:* 283
  concave, *A: 2:* 274
  convex, *A: 2:* 274
Leo (constellation)
  A: 1: 11
Leonardo module (Italian ISS
    component)
  B: 111
Leonov, Aleksei
  A: 1: 148, 148 (ill.), 149, 163;
    2: 198–205, 199 (ill.)

M

Macedon
  A: 1: 21–23
Machu Picchu
  A: 2: 277
Magee, John Gillespie, Jr.
  PS: 141
Magellan spacecraft
  A: 2: 264, 346
Magnetic field, *A: 1:* 120
  defined, *A: 2:* 335
Magnetism, defined
  A: 1: 108
Magnetite globules, in Mars me-
    teorite
  PS: 161
Magnetosphere, defined
  A: 2: 335
Magnifying glasses
  A: 2: 278
*al-Majisti (Almagest; The Greatest;
    The Mathematical Compila-
    tion; He mathematike syn-
    taxis)* (Ptolemy)
  A: 1: 30
"Making Science Make Sense"
    (Jemison)
  B: 118
Malina, Frank J.
  B: 85
Mallory, George
  PS: 58
Malyshev, Yuri
  A: 2: 215 (ill.)
**"Man on the Moon: The Jour-
    ney"** (von Braun)
  PS: 27–37
"Man and the Moon" (TV show)
  A: 1: 110
"Man in Space" (TV show)
  A: 1: 110
*Man into Space (Menschen im
    Weltraum)* (Oberth)
  B: 161
Manhattan Project
  A: 1: 97–98
  PS: 52
Manned Maneuvering Unit
    (MMU)
  A: 2: 254
Manned spaceflight, *A:
    1:* 128–59; *2:* 189. *See also*

Project Apollo; Project
    Gemini; Project Mercury
  basic technology for, *B:* 13,
    72, 159
  Fletcher, James, on, *PS:*
    116–25
  founders of, *B:* 79, 156, 188
  physiological effects of, *B:*
    118, 119, 197
  private enterprise and, *PS:*
    201
  Soviet program for, *A: 1:* 117,
    133–37; *B:* 63–67; *PS:* 43,
    46
  U.S. program for, *A: 1:* 127,
    139–46; *2:* 189, 248–49,
    318–19; *PS:* 60–64, 91, 123
Mao Zedong
  A: 1: 101
Mariner space probes, *A:
    2:* 342–43, 343 (ill.)
  Mariner 2, A: 2: 344
  Mariner 3, A: 2: 347
  Mariner 4, A: 2: 347–48
  Mariner 6 and 7, A: 2: 348
  Mariner 9, A: 2: 348–49
  Mariner 10, A: 2: 342,
    343 (ill.)
Mars, *A: 2:* 347–53
  inspires Robert H. Goddard,
    B: 81
  Kepler, Johannes, and, *A:
    1:* 38
  as seen by Hubble Space Tele-
    scope, *B:* 100, 101 (ill.)
"Mars and Beyond" (TV show)
  A: 1: 110
Mars Climate Orbiter space probe
  A: 2: 350–51
Mars exploration
  Mars Exploration Program, *A:
    2:* 349, 351–53; *PS:* 171
  Mars Global Surveyor, *A:
    2:* 349, 352 (ill.); *PS:*
    171–72
  Rover Mission, *A: 2:* 351–53
  Spirit rover, *PS:* 195
  visions of, *B:* 8, 58–60,
    134–35
  von Braun on future of, *PS:*
    25, 38
Mars Express space probe
  A: 2: 351

Mars Global Surveyor space probe
  A: 2: 349, 352 (ill.)
  PS: 171–72
Mars meteorite
  PS: 160–62, 161 (ill.), 164,
    167 (ill.)
Mars Odyssey space probe
  A: 2: 351
Mars 1–5 space probes
  A: 2: 347
Mars Pathfinder space probe
  A: 2: 349–50
Mars Polar Lander space probe
  A: 2: 350–51
The Mars Project (von Braun)
  B: 201
  PS: 25
Mars rovers
  A: 2: 349–50, 352–53
  PS: 171
Marshall Islands
  A: 1: 99
Marshall Space Flight Center
  A: 1: 126
Marsnik probes
  A: 1: 119
Martians
  A: 1: 100
Marx, Karl
  A: 1: 89–90
Mass, *A: 1:* 53
  defined, *A: 1:* 48, 163
Materials Science
  A: 2: 233
Math and science education
  Jemison, Mae, and, *B:* 118–20
  Ride, Sally, and, *B:* 176–78
*The Mathematical Compilation
    (He mathematike syntaxis; al-
    Majisti; Almagest; The Great-
    est)* (Ptolemy)
  A: 1: 30
*Mathematical Principles of Natural
    Philosophy (Philosophiae Nat-
    uralis Principia Mathematica)*
    (Newton)
  A: 1: 42
Mathematicians
  Aristarchus of Samos, *A:
    1:* 26–27
  Galileo (Galileo Galilei), *A:
    1:* 38–41, 40 (ill.)
  Kepler, Johannes, *A: 1:* 37
    (ill.), 37–38

Newton, Isaac, *A: 1:* 41 (ill.), 41–43, 53, 60 (ill.), 66
Pythagoras, *A: 1:* 25
Mattingly, Thomas K., II
  A: 1: 182
Mauna Kea, Hawaii
  A: 2: 286, 297
Maxwell, James Clerk
  A: 1: 64
Mayan people, and El Caracol
  A: 1: 17–19
Mayans
  A: 2: 277
McAuliffe, Christa
  A: 1: 175; *2:* 256, 256 (ill.)
  B: 43, 43 (ill.), 46, 47
  PS: 133–36, 134 (ill.), 136 (ill.), 137, 138, 139
McCandless II, Bruce
  B: 99
McCarthy, Joseph R.
  A: 1: 102–4, 103 (ill.)
McCarthyism
  A: 1: 102–4
McClellan, George B.
  A: 1: 57
McConnell, Malcolm
  B: 8–9
McCool, William C.
  A: 1: 175; *2:* 266
  PS: 178, 179 (ill.)
McDivitt, James A
  A: 1: 152, 177
  B: 16
McDonald Observatory
  A: 2: 298
McNair, Ronald
  A: 1: 175; *2:* 255, 256 (ill.)
  B: 39, 42, 43 (ill.), 45
  PS: 139
Mechanics, celestial, defined
  A: 1: 24
Medallions, commemorative, for Apollo-Soyuz test project
  A: 2: 202–3
Medical testing, in Project Mercury
  PS: 80–88
Melvill, Mike
  A: 1: 151
  PS: 143, 201
Men from Earth (Aldrin and McConnell)
  B: 8–9

Men into Space (Oberth)
  B: 162
Ménière's disease
  B: 74
  PS: 92
Menschen im Weltraum (Man into Space) (Oberth)
  B: 161
Mercury
  A: 2: 342–43
Mercury 7, *A: 1:* 141; *B:* 146–49, 148 (ill.); *PS:* 74, 75, 91
  public introduction of, *PS:* 79
Mercury 13, *A: 1:* 140; *B:* **146–55**, 147 (ill.); *PS:* 73, 74–89
  Cobb leads the way, *B:* 149–50
  list of participants, *B:* 150–51
  women's program canceled, *B:* 152–54; *PS:* 77–78
The Mercury 13: The Untold Story of Thirteen American Women and the Dream of Space Flight (Ackmann)
  B: 152
  PS: 79–86
Mercury spacecraft program, *A: 1:* 141; *PS:* 67 (ill.). *See also* Project Mercury
Mercury Surface, Space Environment, Geochemistry and Ranging (MESSENGER) probe
  A: 2: 342–43
Mercury Theater
  A: 1: 100
  B: 210
  PS: 4
Mercury-Atlas rocket
  A: 1: 142
Mercury-Atlas 6 spacecraft. *See Friendship 7*
Mercury-Redstone rocket
  A: 1: 142
MESSENGER probe. *See* Mercury Surface, Space Environment, Geochemistry and Ranging (MESSENGER) probe
"Meteor bumper," von Braun, Wernher, envisions
  PS: 33

Meteor Crater (Arizona)
  A: 2: 341
Meteorite, believed to be from Mars
  PS: 160–62, 161 (ill.), 164, 167 (ill.)
Meteorite, defined
  A: 1: 108–9
Meteoroid shield, of Skylab
  A: 2: 218–20
A Method of Reaching Extreme Altitudes (Goddard)
  A: 1: 71
  B: 83
  PS: 14–19
Metz, France
  A: 2: 201
Mexico, El Caracol
  A: 1: 17–19
Mexico, Morelos satellite
  B: 139
Meyer, Patrick, *PS:* 145–59
  "Living on *Mir:* An Interview with Dr. Shannon Lucid," *PS:* 149–56
Microgravity, *A: 2:* 222
  defined, *A: 2:* 210, 239
  effect of on humans, *A: 2:* 233
Microgravity Payload (U.S.)
  B: 56
Micrometeorite, *A: 1:* 120
  defined, *A: 1:* 108–9
Microsatellite
  A: 2: 327
Microvariability and Oscillations of Stars (MOST)
  A: 2: 327
Microwave radiation
  A: 2: 303
Microwaves, *A: 2:* 303, 306 (ill.)
  defined, *A: 2:* 304–5
Middle Ages
  A: 1: 32
Military applications
  of rocket research, *A: 1:* 79–80, 98; *B:* 83, 85, 195, 197–200; *PS:* 12
  of space shuttle, *PS:* 122
Military jet test pilots, NASA preference for
  B: 148–49
  PS: 69, 75, 86

Military rockets
    American use, *A: 1:* 45–47, 46
        (ill.), 55–57
    European use, *A: 1:* 50–55
Milky Way galaxy
    A: 1: 1–2; *2:* 295
    B: 97
Mind at the End of its Tether
        (Wells)
    B: 212
Minorities and women
    astronaut firsts, *B:* 37
    astronaut training for, *B:*
        34–35, 36–39, 152–53; *PS:*
        85
Minuteman intercontinental
        ballistic missile (ICBM)
    A: 1: 98
Mir space station, *A: 2:* 222–29,
        223 (ill.); *B:* 57, 107–8; *PS:*
        47, 147 (ill.)
    astrophysics research labora-
        tory, *A: 2:* 224
    civilian visitors to, *PS:* 156
    components of, *A: 2:* 223–26
    continued problems on, *A:*
        2: 226–29
    cost of, *A: 2:* 226
    dimensions of, *A: 2:* 226
    Haigneré, Jean-Pierre, and, *B:*
        90, 90 (ill.)
    Kristall module, *A: 2:* 224–25
    Kvant 1 module, *A: 2:* 224
    Kvant 2 module, *A: 2:* 224
    letter from *Mir* (excerpt), *B:*
        143
    Lucid, Shannon, and, *B:*
        141–44, 142 (ill.); *PS:* 146
        (ill.), 146–57, 152 (ill.)
    mishaps, *A: 2:* 226–28
    Priroda module, *A: 2:* 225
    Spektr module, *A: 2:* 225
    U.S. astronauts on, *A: 2:* 225
Mir 2
    B: 108
Mirrors
    of Hubble Space Telescope, *A:*
        2: 315; *B:* 95–96, 99, 100
    in reflecting telescopes, *A:*
        2: 286
MISS project
    PS: 68
Missile, ballistic
    defined, *A: 1:* 108, 130

Korolev, Sergei, and, *PS:* 42,
        46
Mission specialist
    first, *B:* 114, 116
    of space shuttle, *A: 2:* 238
Mitchell, Edgar
    A: 1: 181
    B: 74
    PS: 92
Mittelwerk
    B: 198, 199
    PS: 26
MMU. *See* Manned Maneuvering
        Unit (MMU)
Modules, of spacecraft. *See* spe-
        cific modules
Mohler, Stanley
    PS: 81
Molly Brown spacecraft
    B: 14
Mongols, and fire arrows
    A: 1: 50
Moon, *A: 1:* 3; *2:* 331, 334–42
    ancient Greeks and, *A:*
        1: 25–31
    El Caracol and, *A: 1:* 18 (ill.),
        19
    distance from Earth, *A: 1:* 29
    far side, *A: 2:* 337
    first orbit of, *A: 1:* 176–77
    Galileo and, *A: 1:* 39
    search for ice on, *A: 2:* 340–41
    space race to, *A: 1:* 163, 179
    Stonehenge and, *A: 1:* 16
        (ill.), 17
The Moon Car (Das Mondauto)
        (Oberth)
    B: 161
Moon exploration
    future of, *B:* 21
    Kennedy on, *PS:* 50–58
    Kraft, Christopher, on future
        of, *B:* 134–35
    Oberth, Hermann, contribu-
        tions to, *B:* 162
    Tsiolkovsky, Konstantin, vi-
        sion of, *B:* 192
    U.S. plans for, *PS:* 196
    von Braun on future of,
        PS: 24–37
Moon flight, first manned
    B: 133–34
    PS: 109

Moon landing, *A: 1:* 178–84;
        2: 189; *B:* 4–6, 26–30, 29
        (ill.), 133–34; *PS:* 54 (ill.),
        107
    Aldrin, Buzz, *PS:* 110–12
    Armstrong, Neil, *PS:* 110–11
    Bush, George W., on future
        of, *A: 2:* 269
    von Braun, Wernher, envi-
        sions, *PS:* 27–29, 36–37
Moon, Michael Collins's view of
    PS: 108–9
Moon missions. *See also* Project
        Apollo
    Soviet, *A: 2:* 191–92; *B:* 125
    U.S., *A: 1:* 177–80; *PS:* 58
Moon rock
    A: 1: 182; *2:* 339
"Moon rocket," Goddard,
        Robert H.
    A: 1: 72
    B: 83
Moon walks
    A: 1: 178–79, 182
    B: 4–6, 28–30
Moonlet, defined
    A: 2: 335
Morelos satellite (Mexico)
    B: 139
Morgan, Barbara
    PS: 135
"Morning star." *See* Venus
Morton Thiokol
    A: 2: 257, 260–61
    B: 47, 49
    PS: 137, 141–42
MOST. *See* Microvariability and
        Oscillations of Stars
        (MOST)
Motion, Newton's three laws of
    A: 1: 42, 53
Motion sickness. *See also* Space
        adaptation syndrome; Space
        motion sickness
    B: 117
Mount Wilson Observatory,
        A: 2: 293–94; *B:* 97
    Hubble, Edwin, at, *A:*
        2: 294–95
Multiseat spacecraft
    A: 1: 147
Multistage rocket
    A: 1: 68–69

Mysterium cosmographicum (Mystery of the Universe)
(Kepler)
A: 1: 37–38
The Mystery of Mars (Ride)
B: 178

N

N-1 rocket
A: 1: 165–66; *2:* 189
NACA. *See* National Advisory
Committee for Aeronautics
(NACA)
Nagasaki, Japan
A: 1: 97
Naked eye, in stargazing
A: 2: 277
Napoleonic Wars
A: 1: 55
NAS. *See* National Academy of
Science (NAS)
NASA. *See* National Aeronautics
and Space Administration
(NASA)
NASA administrators, Armstrong, Neil
B: 30–31
"NASA Document III-31: The
Space Shuttle" (Fletcher)
PS: 118–24
National Academy of Science
(NAS)
B: 102
National Advisory Committee
for Aeronautics (NACA)
A: 1: 125
B: 24
PS: 47, 60, 68
**National Aeronautics and
Space Administration
(NASA),** *A: 1:* 124–27; *PS:*
160–74. *See also* International Space Station (ISS);
Project Apollo; Project
Gemini; Project Mercury
after Project Apollo, *A: 2:* 191
ambitious schedule precedes
disaster, *A: 2:* 254–55; *PS:*
137–38
astronaut training program, *B:*
3–4, 26–28, 34–35, 36–39,
146–55

budget for, *A: 2:* 217, 249; *PS:*
199
cancels women's Mercury program, *B:* 152–53; *PS:* 77–78
Challenger launch, *A:*
2: 255–59, 258 (ill.); *B:*
46–47, 49–50; *PS:* 136–38
Columbia space shuttle disaster, *PS:* 175–87
creation of, *A: 1:* 82–83,
124–27; *B:* 13, 22, 71–72,
106, 128, 146, 202; *PS:* 37,
43, 60, 68, 74–75, 102, 188
educational outreach and, *PS:*
163, 168–70, 171
excerpts from *The Space Science Enterprise Strategic Plan:
Origins, Evolution, and Destiny of the Cosmos and Life,*
PS: 160–74
and Hubble Space Telescope,
B: 102
International Space Station
(ISS), *A: 2:* 229–30
investigation into *Apollo 1*
fire, *A: 1:* 173; *B:* 19–20
investigation into *Challenger*
launch, *A: 2:* 259–62; *B:* 42,
49–50
investigation into *Columbia*
disaster, *A: 2:* 239, 267–70;
B: 111–12; *PS:* 141–42,
178–85
and Kraft, Christopher, *B:*
128–35
manned space flight program,
B: 147–49; *PS:* 56
and Mars meteorite, *PS:*
160–62, 161 (ill.), 167 (ill.)
"NASA Document III-31: The
Space Shuttle" (Fletcher),
PS: 118–24
Office of Exploration, *B:* 175
Origins Initiative, *PS:* 162–72
race to the moon, *A:*
1: 163–64
revitalization of, *A: 2:* 269–70;
PS: 192–99, 200–1
and Ride, Sally, *B:* 172, 176
Rogers Commission, *A:*
2: 259–62
safety precautions, *B:* 19–20,
50, 112; *PS:* 180

safety record, *PS:* 175–76
setbacks after disasters, *B:*
49–50, 102
space probes program, *A:*
2: 339–41, 342–43, 345,
346, 347, 349–53
space shuttle program, *A:*
2: 238–39, 248–51, 268–70;
PS: 116–31
Space Shuttle Upgrade Program, *A: 2:* 265
space station program, *A:*
1: 124–27; *2:* 211–13
space-based observatories, *A:*
2: 307, 309–10, 314, 315,
319, 321, 324, 328–29
Teacher in Space program, *A:*
2: 256–57
and U.S. Air Force, *PS:* 129
and Vietnam War, *A: 2:* 217
von Braun, Wernher, *A:*
1: 81–83; *B:* 202
National Center for Space Studies (CNES)
B: 89
National Defense Education Act
A: 1: 132
National Socialist German Workers' Party. *See* Nazi Party
Native American astronaut, Herrington, John Bennett
B: 37
Native Americans
names for constellations, *A:*
1: 14
wall calendars, *A: 2:* 277
Natural science, defined
A: 1: 108–9
Nauchnoye Obozreniye (Science Review) (Russian journal)
A: 1: 66
Nazi Party, *A: 1:* 93; *B:* 197–99
and von Braun, Wernher, *A:*
1: 79–81; *B:* 199
NEAR. *See* Near Earth Asteroid
Rendezvous (NEAR)
Near Earth Asteroid Rendezvous
(NEAR)
A: 2: 332 (ill.)
NEAR Shoemaker space probe
A: 2: 362–63
Nebulae
A: 2: 284–85

Onizuka, Ellison S.
  A: 1: 175; *2:* 255, 256 (ill.)
  B: 37, 42, 43 (ill.)
  PS: 139
Onufrienko, Yuri
  A: 2: 227 (ill.)
  B: 141, 142 (ill.)
  PS: 148
Oort, Jan
  A: 2: 290
Opportunity Mars rover
  A: 2: 352–53
Optical radiation
  A: 2: 273, 301, 306, 306 (ill.)
Optical telescopes, *A: 2:* 278,
    293–99
  largest, *A: 2:* 297
  refracting, largest, *A: 2:* 289
Optics, adaptive
  A: 2: 287
Opus Majus (Great Work) (Bacon)
  A: 1: 50
Orbit
  elliptical, *A: 2:* 323
  first U.S., *B:* 72–75
  geosynchronous, *A: 2:* 304,
    310
Orbital Astronomical Observato-
    ries (OAOs)
  B: 98
Orbital flights, Mercury project
  PS: 62, 91
Orbital module (Apollo-Soyuz)
  A: 2: 188 (ill.)
Orbital module, of *Shenzhou 5*
  B: 217
Orbital rendezvous, Gemini
    project
Orbital Workshop (OWS), of
  Skylab, A: 2: 217–18,
    221–22
Orbiter, delta-winged, of space
    shuttle
  A: 2: 239–41, 240 (ill.), 243
    (ill.), 244–48, 248 (ill.)
Orbiter 1
  A: 2: 338 (ill.)
Orbiting Astronomical Observa-
    tories (OAO)
  A: 2: 309
Orbits, Newton's laws and
  A: 1: 43
Orbits, of space shuttle
  PS: 98–99

Origins Initiative, *PS:* 162–70
  goal statement, *PS:* 162–63
O-rings, on shuttle booster rock-
    ets
  A: 2: 257, 260–61
  B: 47, 49, 175
  PS: 137, 141–42
Orion (constellation)
  A: 1: 11
Orléans, France
  A: 1: 51, 52 (ill.)
Osheroff, Douglas
  B: 176
Osiander, Andreas
  A: 1: 34–35
OSS (Office of Space Science)
  PS: 162
Oswald, Stephen S.
  B: 99
Outline of History (Wells)
  B: 211
OV-101 (first space shuttle or-
    biter)
  A: 2: 251
Overwhelmingly Large Tele-
    scope (OWL)
  A: 2: 299
OWL. *See* Overwhelmingly Large
    Telescope (OWL)
OWS. *See* Orbital Workshop
    (OWS)
Oxidizing agents, in rockets
  A: 1: 48, 67
Oxygen, in *Apollo 1* fire
  B: 19
Oxygen, liquid
  A: 1: 67; *2:* 242
Ozone layer, *A: 2:* 306
  defined, *A: 2:* 305

P

Padalka, Gennady I.
  PS: 157, 200
PAHs (polycyclic aromatic hy-
    drocarbons)
  PS: 161
Pal, George
  A: 1: 100
Palomar Observatory
  A: 2: 272 (ill.), 294

Parachutes, and reentry of Mer-
    cury capsule
  PS: 62–63
Parachutes, for rocket landings
  A: 1: 73
Paranal Observatory
  A: 2: 299
Parsons, William
  A: 2: 284
Particles, in physics
  A: 2: 320
Patents, awarded to Goddard,
    Robert
  A: 1: 71, 74
Pathfinder Mars rover
  PS: 171
Pathfinder test shuttle
  PS: 130
Patsayev, Viktor, *A: 1:* 175;
    2: 192, 213
Patterns in the sky. *See* Constel-
    lations
Payload
  defined, *A: 1:* 130; *2:* 239
  of space shuttle, *A: 2:* 241,
    243 (ill.), 264
Payload specialist, of space shuttle
  A: 2: 238
Peenemünde (Baltic coast)
  A: 1: 79
  B: 161, 198
Pegasus (constellation)
  A: 1: 11
Penzias, Arno
  A: 2: 290
People's Republic of China
  A: 1: 101; *2:* 194, 195, 196
Perigee, defined
  A: 1: 130
Personal hygiene, on *Mir*
  PS: 149–50
Perspiration, and *Skylab* space
    station
  A: 2: 218
Philosophers, Aristotle
  A: 1: 25 (ill.), 25–26
Philosophy (ancient Greek), and
    science
  A: 1: 24–26
Phobos (moon)
  A: 2: 352 (ill.)
Photometer, high-speed, on
    Hubble Space Telescope
  B: 95

Physical science, defined
    A: 1: 108–9
Physicians, Jemison, Mae
    B: 114–20
Physicists
    Goddard, Robert H., *B:* 79–86
    Newton, Isaac, *A: 1:* 41 (ill.),
        41–43, 53, 60 (ill.), 66
Physico-Chemical Society (Russian)
    A: 1: 64
    B: 190
"Physics and Medicine of the
    Upper Atmosphere"
    A: 1: 110
Perseus (French-Russian mission
    to *Mir*)
    B: 91
Philae lander
    A: 2: 362
*Philosophiae Naturalis Principia
    Mathematica (Mathematical
    Principles of Natural Philosophy)* (Newton)
    A: 1: 42
Phobos 1 and *2* space probes
    A: 2: 347
Pilot, of space shuttle
    A: 2: 238
Pilots. *See* Fighter pilots; Test pilots (military)
Pioneer space probe program
    A: 2: 345, 353
Pirs (Pier) (Russian ISS component)
    B: 111
Planck Observatory
    A: 2: 329
Planetary motion
    Aristarchus of Samos, *A:
        1:* 26–27
    Aristotle, *A: 1:* 25 (ill.), 25–26
    Brahe, Tycho, *A: 1:* 35–37
    Copernicus, Nicolaus, *A:
        1:* 33–35
    Eudoxus of Cnidus, *A: 1:* 25
    Kepler, Johannes, *A: 1:* 37–38
    Ptolemaic model (Ptolemaic
        universe), *A: 1:* 29–33
    Ptolemy, *A: 1:* 29–33, 31 (ill.)
Planetoid (Sedna)
    A: 2: 294
Planets, of solar system
    A: 1: 3

Plasma rocket engines, research
    on
    B: 57–58
Plough (constellation)
    A: 1: 15
"Plugs-out" test, of *Apollo 1*
    B: 19
Pluto
    A: 2: 334
Pogue, William R.
    A: 2: 221
Poland
    A: 1: 95
Polaris (North Star; Pole Star), *A:
    1:* 10
    and circumpolar constellations, *A: 1:* 13–14
Polyakov, Valery
    B: 107
    PS: 146
Polycyclic aromatic hydrocarbons (PAHs)
    PS: 161
Ponomaryova, Valentina
    Leonidovna
    B: 184
Pope
    A: 1: 32
Popov, Leonid
    A: 2: 216
Popovich, Pavel
    A: 1: 138; *2:* 214
Potassium nitrate
    A: 1: 67
Potocnik, Herman
    A: 2: 211
Potsdam Conference
    A: 1: 96–97
Precession, *A: 1:* 9, 29 (ill.)
    defined, *A: 1:* 4, 24
    and Hipparchus, *A: 1:* 28
Primary mirror, on Hubble
    Space Telescope
    B: 95, 99, 100
Prime mover
    A: 1: 30
Princeton Experiments Package
    A: 2: 310
Priroda module
    A: 2: 225
Prism
    A: 2: 284
Probes. *See also* Space probes

defined, *A: 1:* 130–31, 163;
    2: 239, 335
space, *A: 2:* 331–65
*The Problem of Space Travel: The
    Rocket Motor (Das Problem
    der Befahrung des Weltraums:
    Der Raketen-motor)* (Potocnik)
    A: 2: 211
Progress resupply vehicle (*Mir*)
    A: 2: 216
    B: 143
    PS: 157
Project Apollo, *A: 1:* 147, 160–85;
    2: 189–90, 191; *B:* 11, 13–14,
    20–21, 133–34, 148; *PS:* 56,
    71–72, 75, 102, 103–8, 189.
    See also Apollo program
    Apollo 1 crew, *A: 1:* 171–73,
        172 (ill.); *B:* 11–20, 133; *PS:*
        71–72
    Apollo 11, A: 1: 178–79; *B:* 1,
        4–6, 26–30, 133–34; *PS:*
        102–8, 189
    Apollo 13, A: 1: 180–81
    Apollo 14, A: 1: 181
    Apollo 15, A: 1: 181–82
    Apollo 16, A: 1: 182
    Apollo 17, A: 1: 182–84, 183
        (ill.)
    Lunar Laser Ranging Experiment, *B:* 31
    missions after *Apollo 1, B:*
        20–21, 133; *PS:* 72
    spacecraft, *A: 1:* 161–71, 168
        (ill.)
Project Bullet
    B: 71
    PS: 90
Project Gemini, *A: 1:* 147,
    150–58, 163; *B:* 13, 148; *PS:*
    56, 71–72, 75, 103, 189
    Gemini 8, B: 26
    Kraft, Christopher, served as
        flight director, *B:* 132
    main objectives of, *A: 1:* 150
    Molly Brown, B: 16
    White, Ed, *B:* 16–17
Project Mercury, *A: 1:* 127,
    139–46; *2:* 13, 71–75, 148
    (ill.); *PS:* 56, 60–64, 61 (ill.),
    68–71, 75, 102–3, 116,
    188–89. *See also* Mercury
    spacecraft program

Atlas-D, *A: 1:* 132; *PS:* 62, 66, 93–94
boosters, of space shuttle, *A: 2:* 243 (ill.), 243–44, 260–61; *PS:* 96–98, 129, 137
Chinese, *B:* 216
in Cold War, *A: 1:* 104–5
Congreve, *A: 1:* 55–56
"cosmic rocket trains," *B:* 192–93
early multistage, *A: 1:* 52
fire arrows as, *A: 1:* 49 (ill.), 49–50
forward motion of, *A: 1:* 53
Goddard's first, *A: 1:* 70, 72; *PS:* 20
Jupiter C, *A: 1:* 81, 82 (ill.), 122; *B:* 201
liquid-fuel, defined, *A: 1:* 48
liquid-propellant, *A: 1:* 67–69, 68 (ill.), 72, 74, 76, 77; *B:* 79, 123, 159, 192 (ill.); *PS:* 13–14, 18 (ill.), 42
military, *A: 1:* 98; *B:* 195; *PS:* 12
multistage, *A: 1:* 52, 68–69
N-1, *A: 1:* 165–66; *2:* 189
plasma engine research, *B:* 57–58
Redstone, *A: 1:* 81, 142; *B:* 201; *PS:* 37, 62, 67 (ill.)
R-7, *B:* 124–25; *PS:* 42–43
Saturn, B: 28, 202; *PS:* 38
Saturn 5, A: 1: 83, 168 (ill.), 168–70, 169 (ill.); *2:* 189; *PS:* 31 (ill.), 38 (ill.), 57 (ill.), 103, 105
solid-fuel, defined, *A: 1:* 48
solid-propellant, *A: 1:* 49, 67, 68 (ill.); *B:* 85, 192 (ill.)
of space shuttle, *A: 2:* 240 (ill.), 242, 243 (ill.)
staged, *A: 1:* 98; *PS:* 103
Tsiolkovsky's early designs, *A: 1:* 65 (ill.)
two-stage liquid, *B:* 124
two-stage powder, *B:* 82
V-2, *A: 1:* 79–81, 80 (ill.); *B:* 124, 161, 197–98, 200 (ill.); *PS:* 26
WAC Corporal, *B:* 85
in warfare, *A: 1:* 45–58, 79–81, 104
word origin, *A: 1:* 51

Rockets to Planetary Space (Oberth) *B:* 196–97
"Rockets' red glare" *A: 1:* 45–47, 46 (ill.)
Rogers Commission, *A: 2:* 259–62; *B:* 49, 50, 175; *PS:* 141–42
Armstrong appointed to, *B:* 32
Rogers, William B. *A: 2:* 259 *B:* 49 *PS:* 141
Roman Catholic Church and astronomy, *A: 1:* 32–35, 40–41
and Galileo, *A: 1:* 40–41
Roman Empire *A: 1:* 31–32
Roman religion, and astronomy *A: 1:* 31–32
Romanian scientist, Oberth, Hermann *B:* 156–63
Romans, and constellations *A: 1:* 8–9
Roosa, Stuart A. *A: 1:* 181
Roosevelt, Franklin D. *A: 1:* 86 (ill.), 89, 92, 94 (ill.), 94–95
Rosetta space probe *A: 2:* 362
Ross, Jerry Lynn *B:* 57
Roswell, New Mexico *A: 1:* 72 *B:* 84 *PS:* 20 (ill.), 21
Rotary rockets *A: 1:* 56
Rover defined, *A: 1:* 163; *2:* 335
Mars, *A: 2:* 349–50, 352–53
Rover nuclear rocket *PS:* 54
Rovers, for Mars exploration *PS:* 171, 186
RP-318 rocket *PS:* 42
R-7 rocket *B:* 124–25 *PS:* 42–43

Rubbish, in space *A: 2:* 236, 360
Rudolph II of Bohemia, Holy Roman Emperor *A: 1:* 37
Russia. *See also* Soviet Union International Space Station, *A: 2:* 233; *B:* 108–11
Mir 2, A: 2: 226–29; *B:* 108
Russian (Bolshevik) Revolution, *A: 1:* 69, 88–90
space stations, *A: 2:* 213–17, 222–26, 230–35
Russian aerospace engineer, Tsiolkovsky, Konstantin *B:* 188–94 *PS:* 40–41, 45
Russian cosmonauts Gagarin, Yuri, *B:* 61–68
Tereshkova, Valentina, *B:* 180–87
Russian engineer, Korolev, Sergei *B:* 121–27
Russian language, in Apollo-Soyuz test project *A: 2:* 198
Russian-made space station module Zarya *B:* 110 (ill.)
Rutan, Burt *A: 1:* 151
Ryumin, Valeri *A: 2:* 216

S

Saint-Simon, Henri *PS:* 2
Sakigake space probe *A: 2:* 361
Salisbury plain, England *A: 1:* 17
Sally Ride Club *B:* 177
Sally Ride Science Festival *B:* 177
SALT. *See* Strategic Arms Limitation Treaty (SALT)
Salyut space stations, *A: 2:* 213–17

Secondary mirror, on Hubble
    Space Telescope
  B: 95
Seddon, Margaret Rhea
  B: 139
Sedna planetoid
  A: 2: 294
See, Elliot M.
  A: 1: 154
Senator, Glenn, John
  B: 69–78
Sensors, on space probes
  A: 2: 333
September 11, 2001
  A: 2: 265–66
Service module (Apollo space-
    craft)
  A: 1: 167
  B: 14
  PS: 103–4
Service module (Apollo-Soyuz)
  A: 2: 188 (ill.)
Service Propulsion System (SPS)
  A: 1: 175
Sevastyanov, Vitali
  A: 2: 215
The Shape of Things to Come (film)
  B: 212
Shatalov, Vladimir A.
  A: 1: 177, 179
Shenzhou 5 spacecraft
  A: 1: 156
  B: 214, 216–17, 218 (ill.)
Shepard, Alan, *A: 1:* 141, 143,
    145 (ill.), 162, 181; *2:* 189;
    B: 72, 74, 74 (ill.), 148 (ill.),
    149; *PS:* 51, 61 (ill.), 62, 63,
    75, 92, 93, 95, 116, 188–89
  first American in space, *B:* 12,
    106, 130–31; *PS:* 51, 63
  Kraft, Christopher, recalls
    flight of, *B:* 130
Shepherd, William M. "Bill"
  A: 2: 234
  B: 110
Shoemaker, Eugene M.
  A: 2: 341, 362
Shoemaker-Levy 9 comet
  A: 2: 317, 341
Shonin, Georgi S.
  A: 1: 179
"Should You Be a Rocket Scien-
    tist" (von Braun)
  B: 53

Shuttle Solar Backscatter Ultravi-
    olet Instrument
  B: 54–55, 139–40
Shuttle-*Mir* missions
  A: 2: 226
Shuttles. *See* Space shuttle(s)
Shuttleworth, Mark
  A: 2: 234
Sickle cell anemia
  B: 119
Sidereal day, *A: 1:* 10
  defined, *A: 1:* 4
*Sidereus Nuncius (Starry Messen-
    ger)* (Galileo)
  A: 1: 40; *2:* 280–81
Siemienowicz, Kazimierz, rock-
    etry theory
  A: 1: 53–54
Sight, in stargazing
  A: 2: 277
Sight lines, in ancient observa-
    tories
  A: 2: 277
Sigma 7
  A: 1: 146
  PS: 63
Sinus Roris (Dewy Bay)
  PS: 28–29
Sirius (Dog Star)
  A: 1: 6, 11–13
SIRTF. *See* Space Infrared Tele-
    scope Facility (SIRTF)
67/PChurymov-Gerasimenko
    comet
  A: 2: 362
Sky. *See also* Astronomy
  best, for ground-based obser-
    vatory, *A: 2:* 287
  study of, *A: 2:* 271–76
Sky map, Hipparchus's
  A: 1: 28
Sky powers, worshipped by an-
    cient cultures
  A: 1: 15–19
Skylab space station, *A: 2:* 208
    (ill.), 217–22, 219 (ill.); *PS:*
    146, 153–54
  exercise equipment, *A: 2:* 218,
    221
  experiments, *A: 2:* 220–21
  livable area, *A: 2:* 217–18
  meteoroid shield, *A:*
    2: 218–20

perspiration, *A: 2:* 218
  problems after liftoff, *A:*
    2: 218–19
Slayton, Donald "Deke"
  A: 1: 141; *2:* 198–205, 199
    (ill.)
  B: 148 (ill.), 149
  PS: 61 (ill.), 62, 72, 75
Sleep, on *Mir*
  PS: 150
Sloan, Jerri. *See* Truhill, Jerri
    Sloan
Small Self-Contained Payloads
    (Getaway Specials, or GAS
    payloads)
  B: 139
Smallest space telescope
  A: 2: 327
SMART-1
  A: 2: 341–42
Smith, Michael
  A: 1: 175; *2:* 255, 256 (ill.),
    258
  B: 42, 43 (ill.), 44–45
  PS: 139
Socialism
  of H. G. Wells, *B:* 205,
    211–12
  of Jules Verne, *PS:* 2
Society for Spaceship Travel
  A: 1: 76
  B: 124
Soft landing, defined
  A: 2: 335
SOHO. *See* Solar and Helios-
    pheric Observatory (SOHO)
Sojourner Mars rover
  A: 2: 349–50
Solar and Heliospheric Observa-
    tory (SOHO)
  A: 2: 325–26
Solar arrays, defined
  A: 2: 190
Solar arrays, on Hubble Space
    Telescope
  B: 96, 100
Solar day, *A: 1:* 10, 11
  defined, *A: 1:* 4
Solar eclipses, *A: 1:* 19
  artificial, *A: 2:* 201
Solar flare, *A: 1:* 138
  defined, *A: 1:* 108–9, 130–31;
    2: 210, 305

SPS. *See* Service Propulsion System (SPS)

Sputnik 1, **A: *1:*** 104–8, 114–18, 115 (ill.); **B:** 13, 22, 106, 121, 128, 146–47, 180, 188, 201; **PS:** 37, **40–49**, 41 (ill.), 45 (ill.), 50, 74, 116, 188

  dimensions, **A: *1:*** 115–16

  inspires Franklin Chang-Díaz, **B:** 51–52

  inspires Yuri Gagarin, **B:** 63

  and R-7 rocket, **B:** 125

  series of satellites, **A: *1:*** 117–18, 133

Sputnik 2
  B: 64
  PS: 45–46

Sputnik 3
  A: *1:* 117–18

Sputnik 4 to 10
  A: *1:* 117–18

Spy satellites
  A: *1:* 124–25
  B: 201–2
  PS: 38, 43, 47

"Spyglasses"
  A: *2:* 280

SS *(Schutzstaffel)*
  B: 199
  PS: 26

SS6 rocket
  A: *1:* 119

Stafford, Thomas P.
  A: *1:* 153, 154; *2:* 198–205, 199 (ill.)

Staging, in rocketry
  A: *1:* 68–69, 98

Stalin, Joseph
  A: *1:* 86 (ill.), 89, 92–97, 94 (ill.), 116
  B: 123

Standing stones (Stonehenge)
  A: *1:* 16 (ill.), 17

Stapp, John
  PS: 82

Star (Zvedza) (Russian ISS component)
  B: 110

Star City
  A: *2:* 234

Star Town (Zvezdniy Gorodok)
  B: 63
  PS: 146

Star Trek (TV show)
  A: *2:* 251
  PS: 131

Star Trek: The Next Generation
  B: 120

"Star war events"
  A: *1:* 19

Starcraft Booster, Inc.
  B: 8

Stardust space probe
  A: *2:* 361

Stargazers (ancient), name constellations
  A: *1:* 14–16

Starry Messenger (Sidereus Nunciusr) (Galileo)
  A: *1:* 40; *2:* 280–81

Stars, **A: *1:*** 1–20. *See also* Constellations; specific stars

  binary, defined, **A: *2:*** 304

  composition of, **A: *1:*** 1

  defined, **A: *1:*** 1, 4

  exploding, **A: *2:*** 311–12

  formation of, **A: *2:*** 293

  generate light, **A: *1:*** 3–4

  groups of, **A: *1:*** 7

  Hipparchus's catalog of, **A: *1:*** 28

  infrared observation of, **A: *2:*** 326

  neutron, defined, **A: *2:*** 275, 305

  scale of magnitude (Hipparchus), **A: *1:*** 28

  twinkling of, **A: *1:*** 3–4

"Stars Are Calling" (Tereshkova)
  B: 181

"The Star-Spangled Banner"
  A: *1:* 45–47, 46 (ill.), 56

Steadman, Bernice "B"
  B: 147 (ill.)
  PS: 77, 77 (ill.)

Steam engine
  A: *1:* 47

Stellar nurseries
  A: *2:* 293

Stellar scintillation, **A: *1:*** 3–4
  defined, **A: *1:*** 4

Stellar wind, defined
  A: *2:* 305

Stickless rockets
  A: *1:* 56

Stjerneborg Observatory *(Castle of the Stars)*
  A: *1:* 36

Stock Market Crash (1929)
  A: *1:* 79

Stonehenge
  A: *1:* 16 (ill.), 16–17

Storytelling, and naming constellations
  A: *1:* 14–15

Strategic Arms Limitation Treaty (SALT)
  A: *2:* 196

STS. *See* Space Transportation System (STS)

STS-1 shuttle flight
  A: *2:* 252

STS-5 shuttle flight
  A: *2:* 252–53

STS-26 shuttle flight
  A: *2:* 262

STS-30 shuttle flight
  A: *2:* 264

STS-31 shuttle flight
  A: *2:* 264

STS-34 shuttle flight
  A: *2:* 264

STS-37 shuttle flight
  A: *2:* 264

STS-41 shuttle flight
  A: *2:* 264

STS-50 shuttle flight
  A: *2:* 263–64

STS-51L. *See Challenger*

STS-57 shuttle flight
  A: *2:* 265

STS-93 shuttle flight
  A: *2:* 264

STS-107 shuttle flight. *See also Columbia*
  A: *2:* 266

Stuart, J.E.B.
  A: *1:* 57

Stumbough, Gene Nora. *See* Jessen, Gene Nora

S-turn maneuvers, of shuttle orbiter
  A: *2:* 247

Subaru Telescope
  A: *2:* 297

Suborbital flights, Mercury project
  A: *1:* 142–43

"The Theory of Gasses" (Tsiolkovsky)
A: 1: 63
B: 190
Thermal tiles, of space shuttle
A: 2: 241–42, 250–51
Thermonuclear race. *See also* Cold War
A: 1: 101
The Thing (film)
A: 1: 108
Thiokol. *See* Morton Thiokol
The Third Planet: Exploring the Earth from Space (Ride)
B: 177
Thomas, Andrew
A: 2: 225, 228–29
Throttle up, of space shuttle engines
A: 2: 242, 243
Thrust, *A: 1:* 53
defined, *A: 1:* 48, 130–31, 163; *2:* 239
of space shuttle engines, *A: 2:* 242, 243
Thuban (star)
A: 1: 10
Tiles, thermal
of space shuttle, *A: 2:* 241–42, 250–51
Time
and light, *A: 2:* 299
and position of stars, *A: 1:* 11
and space probe transmissions, *A: 2:* 334
The Time Machine: An Invention (Wells)
B: 206, 208, 209 (ill.)
Titan (moon)
A: 2: 358
Titan II rocket
A: 1: 151
Tito, Dennis
A: 2: 229, 234
Titov, Gherman
A: 1: 137–38
B: 65
To Space and Back (Ride)
B: 177
Tono-Bungay (Wells)
B: 210
Touch-hole, of handgun
A: 1: 51

Toy Story
B: 9
TPF. *See* Terrestrial Planet Finder (TPF)
Tracking and Data-Relay Satellite (TDRS)
A: 2: 255
B: 43, 47, 140
PS: 137
Trajectory (flight path), of spacecraft
PS: 41
Tranquility Base
B: 4–6, 28–30
Travel to the Moon (Verne)
B: 157
Treaty of Brest-Litovsk
A: 1: 90
Treaty of Versailles
B: 197
Tree seeds, for Apollo-Soyuz test project
A: 2: 203
Trigonometry, and Hipparchus
A: 1: 28–29
"Trinity" atomic test
A: 1: 96 (ill.), 97
Trotsky, Leon
A: 1: 91
Truhill, Jerri Sloan
B: 147 (ill.), 151
PS: 77 (ill.)
Truly, Richard
B: 38 (ill.)
Truman, Harry S.
A: 1: 95–96
Trusses, for International Space Station
B: 109, 110, 169
Trypanosoma
B: 58
T-seal, on *Columbia*
PS: 180
Tsien Hsue-Shen
B: 216
Tsiolkovsky, Konstantin, *A: 1:* 63–69, 64 (ill.), 130; *2:* 209; *B:* 188–94, 189 (ill.)
basic rocket formula, *A: 1:* 66, 67
develops theories of space travel, *B:* 191–93; *PS:* 40–41, 45

envisions colonization of space, *B:* 193–94
writes about his ideas, *B:* 190–91
TSKB-39 sharashaka
PS: 42
Tupolev, Sergei
B: 124
PS: 42
Twenty Thousand Leagues Under the Sea (Verne)
A: 1: 62
PS: 2
Twin Keck Telescopes
A: 2: 297–98, 298 (ill.)
Twinkling, of stars
A: 1: 3–4
Typical solar wind
A: 2: 364

U

Uhuru satellite
A: 2: 321
UKIRT. *See* United Kingdom Infrared Telescope (UKIRT)
Ultraviolet (UV) radiation, *A: 2:* 273, 306, 306 (ill.)
defined, *A: 1:* 108–9; *2:* 274–75, 305
Ultraviolet (UV) telescopes
A: 2: 309–10
Ulysses probe
A: 2: 363–64
Umar, caliph of Baghdad
A: 1: 24
Underwater astronaut training, *B:* 3
AT&T Telstar satellite, *B:* 139
Cold War space race, *B:* 1, 13, 22, 61, 106, 121, 128, 147, 180, 201
joint space shuttle missions with Russia, *B:* 55, 57
Union of Soviet Socialists Republics (USSR). *See also* Soviet Union
A: 1: 91
Union troops, and Hale rockets
A: 1: 57
United Kingdom
A: 2: 310

Wan Hu
  A: 1: 50
War of 1812
  A: 1: 45–47, 46 (ill.)
War Fortifications (Bellifortis)
    (von Eichstadt)
  A: 1: 51
The War of the Worlds (film)
  A: 1: 100, 108
The War of the Worlds (Wells),
    A: 1: 70, 100; *B:* 206, 210;
    PS: 4
  excerpt, *B:* 211
  inspires Robert H. Goddard,
    B: 81
Warfare rockets, *A: 1:* 45–58
  European use, *A: 1:* 50–55
  fire arrows, *A: 1:* 49 (ill.),
    49–50
  gunpowder for, *A: 1:* 48–49
  in World War II, *A: 1:* 79–80
Wartime rockets
  PS: 12
Water, on Mars
  A: 2: 353
Water vapor
  A: 2: 287, 292
Wavelength, in electromagnetic
    radiation
  A: 2: 273, 301–3
"Wavy particles, in physics"
  A: 2: 320
*Ways to Spaceflight (Wege zur
    Raumschiffahrt)* (Oberth)
  A: 1: 75
  B: 160
Weapons (rockets as), *A:
    1:* 45–58
  in World War II, *A: 1:* 79–81
Weather
  Challenger launch, *A: 2:* 257;
    B: 47; *PS:* 137–38
  satellites for observation, *PS:*
    54–55
Webb, James E.
  A: 2: 328
  PS: 86
Weightlessness
  A: 1: 157–58
  B: 117
  PS: 91, 99
Weitz, Paul J.
  A: 2: 220

Welles, Orson
  A: 1: 100
  B: 210
  PS: 4
Wells, H. G., *A: 1:* 78, 100; *B:*
    205–13, 206 (ill.); *PS:* 4
  begins writing career, *B:*
    208–10
  inspires rocket scientists, *A:
    1:* 70
  promotes worldwide social-
    ism, *B:* 210–12
West Germany
  A: 1: 101
Western civilization, exploration
    and
  A: 1: 59–61
Weyprecht, Karl
  A: 1: 111–12
When Worlds Collide (film)
  A: 1: 108
Whipple, Fred
  PS: 29
White dwarfs
  A: 2: 322
White, Edward, *A: 1:* 152;
    2: 360; *B:* 11, 12 (ill.),
    16–17, 17 (ill.), 133; *PS:* 72,
    104. *See also Apollo 1* crew
  dies in *Apollo/Saturn 204*
    spacecraft fire, *A: 1:* 171–73,
    175
White Knight (jet plane)
  A: 1: 151
  PS: 201
White, Robert
  PS: 70
Wide-field planetary camera, on
    Hubble Space Telescope
  B: 95, 96, 100
Wild 2 comet
  A: 2: 361
Wilkinson Microwave
    Anisotropy Probe (WMAP)
  A: 2: 314
Williams, Jim
  B: 31
Wilson, Robert
  A: 2: 290
Wilson, Woodrow
  A: 1: 90, 92 (ill.)
Wind tunnel, first Russian
  A: 1: 64

  B: 191
  PS: 41
Winter solstice
  A: 1: 16
WMAP. *See* Wilkinson Mi-
    crowave Anisotropy Probe
    (WMAP)
Wolf, David
  A: 2: 225
Wolfe, Tom, *PS:* 60–73, 64 (ill.)
  excerpts from *The Right Stuff,*
    PS: 65–71
Woltman, Rhea Allison
  B: 151, 152
  PS: 76–77
Women and minorities
  astronaut firsts, *B:* 37
  astronaut training for, *B:*
    34–35, 36–39, 152–53, 174;
    PS: 85
Women astronauts, *PS:* 75–78,
    83 (ill.), 87 (ill.)
  advantages over men, *PS:*
    79–80
  Chinese, *B:* 219
  Collins, Eileen, *B:* 154
  Cowings, Patricia, *B:* 119
  Lucid, Shannon, *B:* 136–45
  Mercury 13 train as, *B:* 146–55,
    147 (ill.); *PS:* 73, 75–78
  Ochoa, Ellen, *B:* 164–71
  Resnick, Judith, *B:* 42, 43 (ill.)
  Ride, Sally, *B:* 37, 172–79
  Tereshkova, Valentina, *B:*
    180–87
"Women in Space" (Tereshkova)
  B: 186
*Woman on the Moon (Frau im
    Mond)* (film)
  A: 1: 76
  B: 160
Worchester Polytechnic Institute
  PS: 12–13
Worden, Alfred M.
  A: 1: 182
World Sickle Cell Foundation
  B: 119
World socialism, Wells' view of
  B: 211–12
World War I
  Goddard, Robert H., *A: 1:* 71;
    B: 82–83; *PS:* 13

Oberth, Hermann, *A: 1:* 74; *B:*
158
Russia and, *A: 1:* 88–89
World War II
development of atomic bomb,
A: 1: 87, 97–98; *PS:* 52
Gagarin, Yuri, *B:* 62
Glenn, John, *B:* 70–71; *PS:* 90
Goddard, Robert, *A: 1:* 70
Korolev, Sergei, *B:* 124
Oberth, Hermann, *A:*
1: 77–78; *B:* 160–61
von Braun, Wernher, *A:*
1: 79–81; *B:* 197–99; *PS:* 24,
26
Wells, H. G., *B:* 212
Wright-Patterson Air Force Base
PS: 80
A Wrinkle in Time (L'Engle)
B: 115
Writers
Aldrin, Buzz, *B:* 1–10, 9 (ill.)
Oberth, Hermann, *A: 1:* 75; *B:*
159–61
Ride, Sally, *B:* 177–78
Tsiolkovsky, Konstantin, *B:*
193–94
Verne, Jules, *A: 1:* 61–62, 64,
70
Wells, H. G., *B:* 205–13
*Wu-ching Tsung-yao (Complete
compendium of Military Clas-
sics), A: 1:* 49

X

X rays, *A: 2:* 273, 306 (ill.),
306–7, 329
Compton effect, *A: 2:* 320

defined, *A: 1:* 108–9; *2:* 275,
305
X-15 rocket plane
B: 24
PS: 67, 68
X-1B rocket plane
A: 1: 165 (ill.)
B: 25–26

Y

Yalta Conference
A: 1: 86 (ill.), 89, 94 (ill.),
94–95
Yang Liwei
A: 1: 156
B: **214–19**, 215 (ill.)
Yangel, Mikhail
A: 1: 119
Yeager, Chuck
A: 1: 141
PS: 68
Years, *A: 1:* 10
star shift during, *A: 1:* 11
Yegorov, Boris
A: 1: 149
Yeliseyev, Aleksei S.
A: 1: 177, 179
Yerkes telescope
A: 2: 286
Yohkoh satellite observatory
A: 2: 328
Young, John W.
A: 1: 151, 155, 163, 182;
2: 252
B: 16

Youngest American sent into
orbit
B: 172
Yuhangyuan
A: 1: 128

Z

Zarya (Sunrise) (Russian ISS
component)
B: 108, 110 (ill.)
Zarya control module, of Inter-
national Space Station
A: 2: 233
Zero gravity, and space tourism
B: 8
Zero gravity, effect of on hu-
mans
A: 2: 233
Zero gravity, on *Mir*
PS: 151
Zholobov, Vitali
A: 2: 216
Zodiac signs, ancient Egyptian
A: 1: 22 (ill.)
Zond space probe series (Soviet)
A: 2: 339
Zvedza (Star) (Russian ISS com-
ponent)
B: 110
Zvezda service module, of Inter-
national Space Station
A: 2: 233
Zvezdniy Gorodok (Star Town)
B: 63
Zwicky, Fritz
A: 2: 297